Dedication from the original edition of BORSTAL BOY

Do Mo Bh.

BRENDAN BEHAN'S

BORSTAL BOY

ADAPTED FOR THE STAGE BY

Frank McMahon

RANDOM HOUSE   NEW YORK

Mrs. Brendan Behan, in her kindness, gave permission for this adaptation. Tomás Mac Anna, artistic director of the Abbey Theatre, endowed it with magic. The Abbey Theatre, Dublin, gave birth to it.

BORSTAL BOY *was first presented on October 10, 1967, at the Abbey Theatre in Dublin. It was first presented in New York City on March 31, 1970, by Michael Mc-Aloney and Burton C. Kaiser, in association with the Abbey Theatre of Dublin, at the Lyceum Theatre, with the following cast:*

BEHAN *(Brendan Behan as an older man)*	Niall Toibin
BRENDAN *(Brendan Behan in his youth)*	Frank Grimes
SHEILA	Patricia McAneny
MRS. GILDEA	Mairin D. O'Sullivan
I.R.A. MEN:	Brendan Fay
	Liam Gannon
	Don Billet
	Michael Cahill
LIVERPOOL LANDLADY	Phyllis Craig
INSPECTOR	John MacKay
DETECTIVE VEREKER	Dean Santoro
SERGEANT	Joseph Warren
CHARLIE MILLWALL	Bruce Heighley
FIRST WARDER, MR. WHITBREAD	Francis Bethencourt
SECOND WARDER, MR. HOLMES	Arthur Roberts
CALLAN	Liam Gannon
TUBBY	Kenneth McMillan
PRISON CHAPLAIN	Stephen Scott
LIBRARY WARDER	Brendan Fay
BROWNY	Terry Lomax
DALE	James Woods
JAMES	Drout Miller

PRISON GOVERNOR	John MacKay
VOICE OF JUDGE	Brendan Fay
WELSH WARDER, MR. HACKNELL	Arthur Roberts
GOVERNOR OF THE BORSTAL	Stephen Scott
WARDER O'SHEA	Joseph Warren
PRIEST	Don Perkins
COOK	Kenneth McMillan
IMMIGRATION MAN	Brendan Fay
WARDER'S WIFE	Amy Burke
HARTY	Norman Allen
JOE	Drout Miller
JOCK	Don Billet
RIVERS	Liam Gannon
SHAGGY	Terry Lomax
CRAGG	Dean Santoro
CHEWLIPS	Michael Cahill
TOM MEADOWS	James Woods
KEN JONES	George Connolly

CROWDS, NEWSBOYS, POLICEMEN, OTHER WARDERS, ETC.:
Tom Signorelli, Richard Yesso, Marilyn Crawley,
Richard Yanko, Roslyn Dickens, Peter Hock

Production directed and designed by Tomás Mac Anna
Associate Producer Joyce Sloane
Set supervision and lighting by Neil Peter Jampolis
Costume supervision by Robert Fletcher
Production Stage Manager William Ross

SYNOPSIS OF SCENES

ACT ONE

The many scenes begin in the streets of Liverpool in the summer of 1939, when the Irish Republican Army was engaged in its bombing campaign to free Northern Ireland; then to Dublin, and back to Liverpool—to a boarding house, Walton Jail, and the Liverpool court.

ACT TWO

Most of the action takes place at Hollesley Bay, a boys' Borstal (detention home for juvenile delinquents) in England. The final scenes take place aboard a ship headed for Ireland and on the Dublin quayside.

ACT
one

As the curtain rises, a portrait of BRENDAN BEHAN *and a solitary cell and bed without mattress come into view. Then the stage goes dark, and the props and scenery are removed.*

BEHAN *(Offstage, singing)*
Oh, listen to me story,
'Tis about a stout young lad
Who up and joined the I.R.A.
Just like his fighting dad,
But all the rebels taught him
With their patriotic talk,
Was to fix a stick o' gelignite
On an oul' alarm clock
(A clock is heard ticking ominously offstage. Suddenly there is an explosion. People are running, screaming and shouting. Police whistles are heard. A crowd gathers. NEWSBOYS *run in)*

NEWSBOYS I.R.A. outrage! Bomb explosion Liverpool! I.R.A. terrorist captured! Another I.R.A. outrage in Liverpool! I.R.A. terrorist injured by his own bomb!
(From the outskirts of the crowd, a familiar figure comes forward to address the audience. It is the elder BRENDAN BEHAN. *The crowd clears the stage)*

BEHAN That poor fellow was a Dubliner called Jerry Gildea, a clerk in Guinness' Brewery. He volunteered

3

to go active in England for the period of his summer holidays—a fast whip over via the boat, a time bomb planted in a railway or a dock warehouse and back to the office. Begod there's many a man became a Senator for less. But the inscrutable ways of the Lord being what they are, the first day he was in Liverpool an incendiary primer exploded in his pocket, and with half his face burned off he was savaged and nearly lynched by the populace, who apparently disapproved of having the dump burned about their ears. *(Young* BRENDAN BEHAN *enters and is caught in an early morning shaft of sunlight)* At that time I was being trained in an old castle the I.R.A. had taken over at Killiney, near Bernard Shaw's cottage, looking away over the Irish Sea. Shaw said that no man was ever the same after seeing it at dawn or sunset. You could sing that if you had an air to it. I know a good many besides meself that are not the same after seeing it, some of them being hung or shot or gone mad, or otherwise unable to tell the difference. Anyway, I was detailed to break the news to Gildea's mother . . . His cousin escorted me to the house. A lovely girl—just my weight, in fact, if I could screw up the courage to try.

(SHEILA, *a young Dublin girl of eighteen, comes in.* BRENDAN *goes to meet her)*

BRENDAN   Hello, Sheila.

SHEILA   Hello. *(After a silence)* Well, come on. *(They walk around)* He got fifteen years.

BRENDAN   There'll be a vacant stool in Guinness' for a while to come.

SHEILA   That's a rotten thing to say. Maybe it'll happen to yourself some day.

BRENDAN   M-m-maybe.

BEHAN   And all the people at home will say, "Ah, sure, God help poor Brendan. Wasn't I only talking to him a week ago. Bejaysus wasn't he a great lad all the same —and he only sixteen!"

SHEILA   *(After another pause)*   It's not in the paper. About Jerry, I mean.

BRENDAN   It's in the paper all right. *(Shows her)* There. Look.

SHEILA   But it says Clarence Rossiter.

BRENDAN   Yeh. All the I.R.A. use mostly Norman names. Could be Irish or English. Like D'Arcy or Dillon.

BEHAN   I knew a Connemara man who christened himself Thomas de Quincey. He could hardly speak English.
   (BRENDAN *and* SHEILA *walk on a little more*)

BRENDAN   We . . . We don't have to rush, do we? I mean, why all the hurry? Such a nice evening.

SHEILA   She was expecting him home today.

BRENDAN   I know.

SHEILA   She doesn't even know Jerry was in the Movement.

BRENDAN   I know. It's going to be v-v-v-very h-h-h-hard.

BEHAN A man needs to keep his heart up in a moment like this. Go on.

>   (BRENDAN *kisses her on the cheek*)

SHEILA That's enough, now. (BRENDAN *grabs her to kiss her again. She breaks away*) You should be ashamed of yourself, and you an I.R.A. man. Especially at a time like this.

BRENDAN Aw, come on, Sheila. Just one.

SHEILA No.

BRENDAN I'll make an awful eejit of meself now, telling his mother . . . You should have let me.

SHEILA What do you take me for? Come on! *(They reach* MRS. GILDEA's *house.* SHEILA *knocks)* She's coming.

MRS. GILDEA (*Comes out*) Sheila. It's nice to see you.

SHEILA Aunty, this is an . . . er . . . friend of mine, Brendan Behan.

MRS. GILDEA You're welcome, Brendan. Come in, both of you, and I'll make you a cup of tea.

BRENDAN Er . . . no . . . n-n-no, ma'am . . . I . . . er . . . never drink tea.

SHEILA Brendan has a message for you, Aunty.

BRENDAN Well . . . no . . . n-n-not exactly . . . er . . .

SHEILA   It's about Jerry. Go on, Brendan. *(Pauses)* Well, go on. Tell her.

BRENDAN   M-m-m-Mrs. Gildea, y-y-your son, J-j-j-Jerry, w-w-was—

MRS. GILDEA *(Easily)*   Yes, lad?

BRENDAN   Y-y-your s-s-son, J-j-j-Jerry—

MRS. GILDEA *(Proceeding to help out)*   Ah, sure, God help us, take your time, son. My son, Jerry, was—?

BRENDAN   H-h-h-he was—

MRS. GILDEA   He was delayed by the boat, was he? Ah, sure, you could expect that this time of year. I'm told the crowds of the world does be in the Isle of Man.

BRENDAN   H-h-h-he w-was—

MRS. GILDEA   Nice place, too, and a nice class of people, be all accounts. Talk Irish, and all, some of them. More nor I could do. Though the cats doesn't have any tails.

BRENDAN *(Desperate)*   He was s-s-s-sen—

MRS. GILDEA   God knows, they must be the queer-looking beasts. Still, everyone to their fancy, as the old one said when she kissed the ass.

BRENDAN *(Catching her by the sleeve)*   H-h-he w-w-was s-s-sent—

7

MRS. GILDEA   God help you, and such a nice boy too. Maybe, it'd be God's Holy Will that you'd grow out of it. Sure, you're not finished growing yet.

BRENDAN   He was s-s-sentenced—

MRS. GILDEA   Sentenced?

BRENDAN *(In a rush)*   To f-fifteen years in Liverpool today.

MRS. GILDEA   Jerry . . . sentenced in Liverpool? . . . But . . .

BRENDAN   He . . . he was . . . in . . . in . . . t-t-t-the I.R.A., Mrs. Gildea. He . . . he had an accident—

MRS. GILDEA   Mother of God!

BRENDAN   H-he w-w-w-was caught, Mrs. Gildea.

MRS. GILDEA   Sweet mother of Jesus, comfort me this night!
   (She goes off, weeping, supported by SHEILA*)*

SHEILA   You could have broken it easier to her, couldn't you?

BRENDAN   Jaysus!
   *(*BRENDAN *stands alone. Four* I.R.A. MEN *in trench coats come to him, one with a suitcase. He opens it)*

I.R.A. MAN   It's all there. Gelignite, detonators, potassium chloride, sulphuric acid. And a brand new alarm clock. Make sure you get rid of them first if there's trouble. Understand?

BRENDAN Yes.

SECOND I.R.A. MAN Travel permit and instructions— in Gaelic. Good luck.

I.R.A. MEN Up the Republic!

BRENDAN Up the Republic!
    (They shake hands with him and leave)

I.R.A. MAN Oh, I nearly forgot. Your ticket.

BRENDAN *(Alone, looking at ticket)* Dublin-Liverpool, third class. One way! Jaysus!
    (BEHAN *sings the song "Old Alarm Clock" as young* BRENDAN *makes his way through crowds of people, as if on the streets of Liverpool. A policeman sees him with his suitcase, and starts to follow him)*

BEHAN *(Sings)*
    When first I came to Liverpool
    In the year of thirty-nine,
    The city looked so wonderful
    And the girls were so divine,
    I walked on air among them
    And of me they did take stock,
    But they didn't see me gelignite
    And me oul' alarm clock.

NEWSBOYS Great victory for Royal Navy! German

battleship scuttled! *Graf Spee* sunk off Argentine!
Great British sea victory!

> *(The crowds are clearing away, and suddenly*
> BRENDAN *is alone in the center of the stage. The*
> *lighting changes to show a room with a bed and*
> *a rickety chair. The* LANDLADY, *a middle-aged,*
> *sharp-featured woman, is making the bed)*

BEHAN *(Singing)*
> Tomorrow down be Cammell Lairds
> If I only get the chance,
> I'll show you how me small machine
> Can make the coppers dance:
> It ticks away politely
> Till you get an awful shock,
> And it ticks away the gelignite
> In me oul' alarm clock.
>
> > *(*BRENDAN *knocks on the door; the* LANDLADY
> > *opens it)*

BRENDAN   My name is Brendan Behan, ma'am!

LANDLADY   Oh, come in, Mr. Behan. You'll be more
than comfortable here, Mr. Behan. But you must remember one thing: one thing all my lodgers must
remember. I shut the hall door every night regularly
at half past ten of the clock, and then we all kneel
down and say the rosary. Being from Ireland, of course
you'll join us. The other lodger always does—wouldn't
miss a night.

BRENDAN   Yes, ma'am.

LANDLADY   Especially the three Hail Marys I always add
for holy purity.

BEHAN   Three Hail Marys for holy purity and the protection of her person and modesty! You'd think half the men in Liverpool were running after her, panting for a lick of her big buck teeth! (*The* INSPECTOR, DETECTIVE VEREKER *and the* SERGEANT *appear and knock on the door*) Get rid of the stuff!

LANDLADY (*Opens the door for the men*)   Oh God, oh Jesus, oh Sacred Heart! Boy! There's gentlemen below to see you!
        (BRENDAN *frantically grabs the suitcase and starts to run with it*)

INSPECTOR   Grab him, the bastud. (*The* DETECTIVE *seizes* BRENDAN. *The* INSPECTOR *opens the case and takes out the clock*) Got a gun, Paddy?

BRENDAN   If I'd have had a gun, you wouldn't have come through that door so shagging easy!

INSPECTOR (*Sighing*)   Turn him over. (*The* DETECTIVE *begins to frisk* BRENDAN *violently*) No, not you, Vereker—Sergeant. (*The* SERGEANT *searches* BRENDAN *efficiently but without fuss, even along the seams of his fly. From an inside pocket, he extracts* BRENDAN'S *money, travel permit, cigarettes and a letter. He hands the letter to the* DETECTIVE)

DETECTIVE   Gaelic! (*Infuriated*)   You bloody bastud, how would you like to see a woman cut in two by a plate-glass window?

BEHAN   Maybe I should have answered, "What about bloody Sunday, when the Black and Tans machine-

gunned a football crowd in our street?" I had it all
ready too, but the old stutter let me down.

SERGEANT Well, Paddy, there are people gathered
'round this house, and I don't think they mean you
any good. (*He snorts*) We'll get you to the Assizes all
right, safe and sound. Take no heed of them. (*He sits
down on the bed with a grunt*) We'll sit here awhile.
(*He indicates to* BRENDAN *to sit beside him*) I wish to
Christ I was your age, Paddy, I'd have something
better to do than throwing bombs around. How old
are you?

BRENDAN I'm sixteen, and I'll be seventeen in Feb-
ruary.

SERGEANT So they sent you over here, you silly little
twerp, while the big shots are in America, going
around spouting and raking in the dollars and living
on the fat of the land.

    (*The* INSPECTOR *takes* BRENDAN's *cigarettes and
tosses them to him*)

INSPECTOR Have a fag, Paddy. They'll take them off
you soon enough in the Walton Prison.

SERGEANT (*Pointing his pipe at the suitcase*) You're a
silly lot of chaps, going on with this. You don't even
know why you're bloody well doing it. It's supposed
to be about partition. Northern Ireland, about the six
counties. Right? (BRENDAN *nods*) Well, I've inter-
viewed a lot of your fellows and God blind old Reilly
if one of them could even name the bloody things.
Not all six, they couldn't. Go on, now, you. The
whole six, mind.

BRENDAN   You want me to name them now?

SERGEANT   Yeah, go on.

BRENDAN *(Slowly)*   Antrim . . . Armagh . . .

SERGEANT   Right, that's two you've got.

BRENDAN   Down . . . Derry . . . Fermanagh and . . .

SERGEANT   Right, five you got. Come on, the last one—

BRENDAN   Down, Derry and Fermanagh and . . .

SERGEANT *(Triumphantly)*   There you are, Paddy, what did I tell you.

BEHAN   I left out County Tyrone, for he was a nice old fellow.

BRENDAN   I'd like to make a statement.

BEHAN   Propaganda for the cause. It would look well at home, too.

SERGEANT *(Taking out a notebook)*   Go on, Paddy.

BRENDAN   My name's not Paddy. My name is Brendan Behan. I came over here to fight for . . . for . . . for . . .
    (The SERGEANT scribbles all this down furiously. The DETECTIVE glares at BRENDAN)

BEHAN   For the Irish Workers' and Small Farmers' Republic.

BRENDAN For the Irish Workers' and Small Farmers' Republic . . .

BEHAN For a full and free life, North and South, and for the removal of the baneful influence of British imperialism from Irish affairs!

BRENDAN For . . . for . . . *(Desperate)* God save Ireland!

SERGEANT Now, what's all this about small farmers? I never seen a small farmer, Irish or English. They're all bloody big fellows with bull's-'eads on 'em, from eating bloody great feeds and drinking cider.

INSPECTOR Look here, Paddy, I'm an Irishman, the same as you. I'm from Cork. Ever heard of the O'Sullivans?

BRENDAN O'Sullivan's a Cork name, sir.

INSPECTOR So it is—but what kind of name is Behan?

BRENDAN It's a very Irish name, sir. Literary family once prominent in South Leinster. From "beach," meaning a bee, one who keeps bees.

INSPECTOR I don't read Irish, Behan, nor do I speak it. A lot of good it would do me if I did.

BEHAN It might help you to read that frigging document.

INSPECTOR I suppose you realize you can go to jail for the best part of your life over this business? One of your crowd is lying under sentence of death in Birmingham. For a cowardly murder.

BRENDAN (*Quietly*) It was no murder.

DETECTIVE It was no murder? (*With mounting anger*) To put a bomb in a crowded street and kill five innocent people? You bloody little—(*He raises his hand to strike*)—I'll give you murder!
  (*The* SERGEANT *and* INSPECTOR *jump forward to restrain him*)

INSPECTOR All right, Vereker!

DETECTIVE (*Regaining control*) All right, Inspector, all right. Don't you come that stuff here, Behan. You're not with your murder-gang pals in Dublin or Belfast now.

INSPECTOR (*Reasonably*) Listen, Behan, you're only a boy, and your leaders are safe home in Ireland, or in America. We don't want to be hard on you, but the only one who can help you is yourself. You need not consider other people. They're not considering you. (*Growing intimate*) But if you tell us where we can lay our hands on more of this stuff in England, we'll go and get it. No questions asked on one side or the other.

BRENDAN I don't know where there is any other stuff in England, sir.

INSPECTOR Listen, Behan, if you're afraid of what will happen to you when you go home, I can tell you this. If you help us, we can look after you. You won't be the cause of anyone being arrested, because we can't make arrests in Ireland. But you help us in stopping this business and, as I say, we'll look after you. *(He pauses to let it sink in)* You're a young man, not even that yet. We'll send you to the colonies, Canada maybe, put you on the boat with money in your pocket. *(Pauses)* Well?

BRENDAN   I can't help you, sir.

INSPECTOR   You mean you won't. Well, you've a long time to go till the Assizes.

SERGEANT   I think we can move now, sir. There ain't so many people outside.

INSPECTOR   Right. Open his buttons. That will keep him quiet. No, not you, Vereker. Sergeant.

   (*The* SERGEANT *undoes* BRENDAN's *pants buttons*)

SERGEANT   That landlady of yours won't have a window left in her house tonight. They'll probably give the lodgers a kicking and all, too.

INSPECTOR   Come on!

SERGEANT   I shouldn't be surprised if they leave the house a wreck.

   (BRENDAN *is lead away. Soon he is moving through a Liverpool crowd, such as we saw earlier, shouting at him in fury*)

CROWD   Filthy murderers! . . . Dirty Irish swine! . . . Kill the bastard! . . . String 'im up!

LANDLADY   Oh, God! Oh, Jesus! Oh, Sacred Heart!
   (Policemen move the crowd along)

CROWD   Hang him, the bastard! . . . Dirty I.R.A. swine!
. . . Burn down the house!

   (The crowd starts to clear away, leaving an empty stage. BRENDAN is handed over to two policemen)

BEHAN *(Sings)*
   Said the judge, "Now, listen here, me man
   And I'll tell you of our plan,
   For you and all your countrymen
   I do not give a damn."

   Said he, "I'm going to charge you
   With possession of this machine,
   And I'm also going to charge you
   With the wearing of the green!"

   Says I to him, "Your Honor,
   It is surely not a crime,
   To try to make oul' Ireland free
   And not before its time!"

   Said he, "When we have done with you,
   You'll be twenty years in dock,
   You can count it by the ticking
   Of your oul' alarm clock."

   (The light is dim. The scene is now the prison lockup. A POLICEMAN and the DETECTIVE bring BRENDAN in. The POLICEMAN hands him to the SECOND WARDER, Mr. Holmes, who is waiting)

POLICEMAN   I.R.A. prisoner, one off to you, sir.

SECOND WARDER Hope he chokes during the bleeding night. Take off them bloody shoes.

(*They throw* BRENDAN *in a cell*)

DETECTIVE You ain't sleeping with the pigs now, you know.

SECOND WARDER Come on, off with them. Look sharp.

(BRENDAN *eyes the two warily*)

DETECTIVE Don't keep the officer waiting here all night, you sloppy Irish pig. You're bloody good soldiers and no mistake. "Up the Republic" outside a boozer on Saturday night. But you won't be long cracking up after a few hours in here.

SECOND WARDER What'll you feel like after twenty year? That's if you're lucky, and they don't 'ang you. Now, off with the jacket. Undo your suspenders.

(BRENDAN *bends slowly to untie his shoelaces, not taking his eyes off the policemen*)

DETECTIVE Give them to the officer.

(BRENDAN *obeys*)

SECOND WARDER You might decide to 'ang yourself in the night. Not that that would be any loss.

DETECTIVE Going to put bombs in the new battleships in Cammell Lairds Shipyards, was you? We didn't do in half enough of you during the Trouble.

BRENDAN I wasn't born the time of the Trouble.

18

DETECTIVE   Well, I got my fill of the I.R.A. and as for
you, you bloody swine, I know what I'd do with you.

BRENDAN   We chased you out of it anyway! You haven't
stopped running yet!
   (*The* DETECTIVE *punches him in the stomach*)

SECOND WARDER   Don't 'eed the dirty little bugger. 'E's
not worth a kick in the arse'ole.

DETECTIVE   One peep out of you during the night, and
the officers will come down and they'll bloody murder
you.

SECOND WARDER   I 'ope 'e gets twenty years. Fecking
little bastard.
   (*They go off*)

BRENDAN   I wish I could wake up and find out I'm only
dreaming this.

BEHAN   Yeh. The way you used to wake up at home and
say, "Well, that's how it would be if I was pinched
in England!"

BRENDAN   And here I am pinched in England.

BEHAN   And this is the way it would be.

BRENDAN   Would be? Is.
   (*He starts to hum*)

BEHAN   That's right. Sing. We never died a winter yet.
   (*Sings*)
Now, this dirty, ugly city

Would put many in the jigs,
The cell it isn't pretty
And it isn't very big,
And I'd long ago have left the place
If only I had got
(BRENDAN *joins in*)
Me couple o' sticks o' gelignite
And me oul' alarm clock.
(There is a blackout. Then a different light comes up. A group of prisoners shuffle in. A title board flies in, saying WALTON PRISON. *It is the next day. There are iron wash troughs onstage.* BRENDAN *joins* CHARLIE, *a youth of seventeen in sailor's uniform, at a trough. One old lag is smoking)*

CHARLIE *(Rubbing his chin)* Could do with a rasp, mate. Been here three days now. They won't let you have your bleedin' razor.

BRENDAN   I only came in last night. I'm not so bad.

CHARLIE   You Irish? (BRENDAN *nods and starts to wash up)* Well, there's a lot of blokes 'round our way that are Irish. We all used to sing Irish songs. Confidentially, I don't like these Lancashire blokes, myself. I'm from London. Smashing place and all, it is, London. Not like Liverpool. Bleeding hole.

BRENDAN   Hole is right.

CHARLIE   I was picked up for some screwing jobs. Here and in Manchester—another bloody graveyard. What are you in for, Pad? Boozer battle or something?

BRENDAN   No, I'm in over the I.R.A. Explosives.

CHARLIE   Are you—

BRENDAN   I am, though.

CHARLIE   Straight up?

BRENDAN   Straight up.

CHARLIE   Cor, you won't half cop it for that lot. Maybe you could say someone gave you the stuff to mind and you didn't know what was in it?

BRENDAN   Maybe. Don't the warders mind the smoking?

CHARLIE   It's got bugger all to do with them.

BRENDAN   They took my cigarettes and matches away from me.

CHARLIE *(Seriously)*   Oh well, Pad, it might be different for you. Being I.R.A., like. It's a sort of 'igh treason, isn't it? But bugger 'em all, china,* you can have some of mine. (BRENDAN *turns away from the washbowl, protesting)* Yes, you bloody will. I'll give you three snout, a card of matches, and a packet of chewing gum. And 'ave you got anything to read?

BRENDAN   No, I haven't.

CHARLIE   Well, I'll give you last week's *News of the World*. *(Taking it out of his pocket)* Though maybe you saw this one?

BRENDAN   *News of the World?* Oh yes, let's see now . . .

* Chum (from cockney rhyming slang: mate—china plate).

21

(Reads) "Hull magistrate on rape charge. Girls of eleven and thirteen—the magistrate was accustomed to giving them free vegetables from his greengrocer's shop."

CHARLIE   Yes! The price of everything's going up.

BRENDAN   No, I haven't seen that issue. Thanks.

CHARLIE   Your hands are wet, Paddy. I'll shove them in your pocket for you—*(He makes a move to put cigarettes into* BRENDAN'*s pants pocket)*—that one's got an 'ole in it. *(He tries the other side)* That's all right. I'll shove the snout, matches and chewing gum in here. (BRENDAN, *his wet hands outstretched, smiles)* And I'll put the paper inside your shirt, so's that old grass'opper won't tumble it. *(Does so)* He won't tumble it there, Paddy, under your shirt.

BRENDAN   Thanks, kid.

CHARLIE   That's all right, kid. And, Paddy, my name is Charlie.

BRENDAN   Thanks, Charlie.

CHARLIE   That's all right, kid . . . I know Irish songs . . . *(He begins to sing the first line of "Galway Bay," then stops and smiles)* . . . and I'll sing you one when we get into the cells. You'll hear me, all right.
      (Mr. Whitbread, the FIRST WARDER, *and Mr. Holmes, the* SECOND WARDER, *come in)*

FIRST WARDER   Answer when your name is called and place your property on the counter. Hartigan!

HARTY   Yes, sir.
(Goes to the counter and empties his pockets)

BRENDAN *(To* CHARLIE*)*   What'll I do with the cigarettes?

CHARLIE   Hold on to what you can. Watch me.

FIRST WARDER   Millwall!

CHARLIE   Here, sir.
(He moves up to the counter)

FIRST WARDER   Smith!

JOCK   Here, sir.
(He goes to the counter)

FIRST WARDER   Callan! *(Roars)* Callan!
*(*SECOND WARDER *grabs* CALLAN *and brings him to the counter)*

CALLAN   Here . . . *(The* FIRST WARDER *shoots him a baleful look)* sir.

FIRST WARDER *(To* SECOND WARDER*)*   Keep an eye on your coat, Mr. 'Olmes. That Irish mick 'as the light touch. Pinched 'Arry Lauder's overcoat from 'is car outside the Alhambra, 'e did. James!

JAMES   Here, sir.
(He goes to the counter)

FIRST WARDER   Bee-han!

BRENDAN   Here, sir.
(He whispers to CHARLIE*)*

FIRST WARDER (*Looking up sharply*) Hey, you, cut out that nattering. You're in prison now, and if you don't want to begin with a dose of bread and water, keep your mouth shut. (BRENDAN *goes to the counter and back. To* SECOND WARDER) Will you turn 'em over, Mr. 'Olmes?

　　(SECOND WARDER *emerges from behind the counter. The prisoners are lined up*)

SECOND WARDER Right, sir. (*He begins with* CHARLIE. *He finds a piece of shoelace and holds it up*) Want to practice sailor's knots or something? (CHARLIE *is sheepish and silent*) Why didn't you 'and it over?

CHARLIE (*Fumbling*) I didn't know.

SECOND WARDER You didn't know *what*?

CHARLIE I didn't know it was any harm.

SECOND WARDER (*Shouting*) You didn't know it was any 'arm, *what*?

CHARLIE Oh, I didn't know, sir. Sir, I didn't know, sir, sorry, sir.
　　(*The* FIRST WARDER *strides up to* CHARLIE *and looks him dead in the eye*)

FIRST WARDER (*Slowly and deliberately*) Remember, when you speak to Mr. 'Olmes in future, you'll 'ave respect and haddress 'im properly.

SECOND WARDER Or any other hofficer of the services, as Mr. Whitbread will tell you. (*The two warders look*

at each other with gravity. SECOND WARDER searches
CALLAN and finds a piece of paper in his pocket. He
holds it up at arm's length for all to see. Sarcastically)
We give you toilet paper 'ere.

CALLAN   I know all about what you give here.
(The SECOND WARDER passes to BRENDAN. He frisks
him and discovers the cigarettes, with some excitement)

SECOND WARDER   What 'ave we got 'ere, eh? (Tensely)
Mr. Whitbread, sir.
(FIRST WARDER comes down and stands by BREN-
DAN. SECOND WARDER holds up the pack of cig-
arettes)

FIRST WARDER (Slightly aghast)   Who 'ad this little lot,
then, Mr. 'Olmes?

SECOND WARDER (Shaken)   This one 'ere, sir. (Thrusts
his face into BRENDAN's) Tell Mr. Whitbread your
name, you.

BRENDAN   B-b-Behan, sir.

SECOND WARDER   Tell Mr. Whitbread your Christian
name.

BRENDAN   Br-br-br-Brendan Behan, sir.

FIRST WARDER (With quiet menace)   Yes, Behan, I've
got you, all right. I.R.A. man, ain't you? Don't like
us much over 'ere, do you, Behan? Pity, you know,
seeing as you're going to spend a long, long time
with us.

SECOND WARDER   About twenty years.

FIRST WARDER   That's what the last got at Manchester, wasn't it? *(He pushes his face closer)* And you was going to blow us all up, Behan? Weren't you, Behan? Weren't you, Behan? *(Shouting)* Weren't you, Behan? Weren't you?

SECOND WARDER *(Reproachfully)*   Answer Mr. Whitbread, Behan.

FIRST WARDER   Not much of the old rebel in you now, is there? Thought you blokes would 'ave brought your ox-guns over with you. Do you know what an ox-gun is, Behan? It's what they 'ave in Ireland for shooting bullshit out of. *(He looks quickly at the others. They laugh, except* CHARLIE *and* CALLAN. CHARLIE'*s face is serious and troubled, but then he too looks away from* BRENDAN *and snickers)* And 'old up your 'ead when I speak to you.

SECOND WARDER   'Old up your 'ead when Mr. Whitbread speaks to you.
     *(*BRENDAN *looks around at* CHARLIE *for an instant)*

FIRST WARDER   What are you looking 'round at, Behan? Look at me.
     *(*BRENDAN *turns his face slowly toward the warder and returns the latter's look steadily)*

BRENDAN *(Quietly)*   I am looking at you.

SECOND WARDER   You are looking at Mr. Whitbread, what?

26

BRENDAN I am looking at Mr. Whitbread.

> (*Mr. Holmes looks gravely at Mr. Whitbread,
> then punches* BRENDAN *in the middle of his back.*
> BRENDAN *reels*)

SECOND WARDER *(Panting)* You are looking at Mr. Whitbread, *what*, Behan?

BRENDAN *(Gasping)* I, sir, please sir, I am looking at Mr. Whitbread, sir.

FIRST WARDER Well, Behan, now you've learned your lesson, remember this: we've only one sort of tobacco 'ere, Three Nuns. None today, none tomorrow, and none the day after. *(The others snicker,* CHARLIE *looking away from* BRENDAN*)* Understand that, Behan?

> (BRENDAN *is still dazed*)

SECOND WARDER Answer Mr. Whitbread, Behan.

BRENDAN Yes—sir. Yes, Mr. Whitbread.

FIRST WARDER Don't you forget it.

BRENDAN *(Beaten)* No, Mr. Whitbread, no, sir.

SECOND WARDER All right, you lot—line up for your uniforms. Look smart now.

> (*They go off.* TUBBY *comes in. He is a prisoner
> in charge of the baths. He is carrying Borstal uni-
> forms, which he distributes to the boys as they
> bathe*)

TUBBY *(Easy and genial)* Don't you go believing anything a copper tells you. It's their *business*—putting the wind up you when they ain't being sweet to you. Like fecking parsons, they are. *(To* BRENDAN*)* Okay, Paddy, like me to rub your back?

BRENDAN *(Smiling)* No, thanks.

TUBBY You'll all go to Borstal, and you'll 'ave a good time, with football . . . concerts . . . swimming . . . Maybe you'll be sent to Portland, where I was. *(They are all ears)* Drake 'Ouse, I was in. Good old Drake! You might even be sent to one of them open Borstals. You give your word of honor not to scarper, and there's no lock on the dormitory door even.

CHARLIE What about Sherwood Forest?

TUBBY That's one place you'd want to stay clear of. First thing when the Sherwood gates shut behind you, you get a poke in the mush from an effing great screw.* 'E'll tell you, "That's for feck all, so just see what you get when you do feck about!" *(*CHARLIE, *who has finished drying himself, has been donning his uniform.* TUBBY *eyes him admiringly)* He'll probably go to Borstal and all. Want to watch his ring-a-ding-a-do, though. *(To* CHARLIE*)* Hey, Jack, any old three-badge stoker ever shown you the golden rivet?

CHARLIE *(Fierce)* I'll show you a knee in your marriage prospects.

TUBBY *(Laughs)* Don't mind me, kid. There's no 'arm in me. Just a bit of good clean fun.

---

* Prison warder.

SECOND WARDER *(Shouts, offstage)* Ready over there?

TUBBY *(Shouting back)* Right, sir! Be right along, sir. *(Dropping his voice)* You fecking shit-'ouse. *(To* BRENDAN*)* Ever 'ear of the screw that married the prostitute? 'E dragged 'er down to 'is own level.
(He explodes with laughter, then composes his face into becoming gravity)

SECOND WARDER *(Offstage)* Hurry up, there!

TUBBY Right, sir! Just coming, sir! *(Smartly, to the boys)* And now, we're 'aving a mannyquin parade.
*(*TUBBY *sashays off, getting a venomous look from* SECOND WARDER *as he enters)*

SECOND WARDER All right, you lot. Stand in line! *(The lights dim to almost total darkness as the boys form up to be marched to their cells. The warder shouts commands; they are marched left and right; keys jangle; they halt.* BRENDAN *keeps moving. They continue to shuffle around in the dark. The lights come up a bit to reveal cells)* Keep moving! Move along! Stand to the door of your cells.
(He throws open cell doors, revealing two tiny cells. The boys start in horror)

BRENDAN *(Entering one cell)* Jaysus! A dwarf's coffin.

CHARLIE *(Entering the other cell)* A bloody hole in the wall.

BRENDAN Smells like a refrigerated lavatory.

SECOND WARDER Silence! Come on, get your bed made down. Don't keep us 'ere all bloody day.
(He slams the door and leaves)

29

BRENDAN *(Surveys the cell, which has a table, a chair, and a bunk that is unmade but has a pile of bedclothes on it. A copy of the regulations hangs on the wall)* All the way back to Dickens.
(He stamps off five paces, wall to wall)

A VOICE *(Offstage)* Hey, you up there!

BRENDAN Yes?

A VOICE *(Offstage)* You rotten sod, kip in. Get on your bloody bench and lay there, you four-footed bastard!

BRENDAN *(A whispered ejaculation)* Jaysus! *(He takes the regulations off the wall and begins reading them. CHARLIE, from the next cell, knocks on the wall. BRENDAN knocks back)*

CHARLIE Hey, Paddy! That you, china?

BRENDAN Hello, Charlie.

CHARLIE Good old Pad. Hey, Pad!

BRENDAN Here, china.

CHARLIE What about that song?

BRENDAN I'll sing you one.
(He puts the regulations on the floor)

CHARLIE Sure. An Irish song. "Mother Machree" or "Galway Bay."

BRENDAN "Mother Machree" me arse! I'll sing a song I

learned at school. *(Grandiloquently)* Ireland weeping for Bonnie Prince Charlie. Not that him or anyone belonging to him ever did anything for us—but it was a good song.

　(He sings)
　Walk, walk, walk, my own,
　Not even God can make us one,
　Now you have left me here alone,
　Is go dtéighidh tú, a mhúirnín, slán.

CHARLIE　Hey, Pad, that last bit's Irish, isn't it?

BRENDAN　Yeah, it's Irish.

CHARLIE　What does it mean?

BRENDAN　What does it mean? It means "May you always be in the palm of God's hand."

CHARLIE　Nick, Pad, nick! They're coming down.
　(Footsteps clump overhead)

BRENDAN *(Frantically)*　They're coming down to me ... Charlie, they could easily kill you in this place. Say you cut up rough. Who'd give a fish's tit about you over here? *(A key jangles; the door swings open)* Into Thy hands, I commend my spirit, Lord Jesus.

FIRST WARDER　You all right in here?

BRENDAN　Smashing, mate.

FIRST WARDER *(Viciously)*　What do you mean *"mate?"* Where the bloody 'ell do you think you are, *"mate?"* And what do you think you're on, putting those regulations on the floor?

BRENDAN   I was only having a read of them, sir.

FIRST WARDER *(Enraged)* Read them where they're supposed to be read—on the wall. Come on, put 'em back.

BRENDAN   Yes, sir.
   (He hastily puts them back)

FIRST WARDER   And what bloody way 'ave you your kit laid out? *(Pointing at the bunk)* Get that bloody lot into shape, or I'll really get angry, you sloppy Irish mick.

BRENDAN   Yes, sir.
   (Bewildered, makes a hopeless stab at doing the bed)

FIRST WARDER *(Shouts)* Millwall! (CHARLIE *comes into* BRENDAN'S *cell.* BRENDAN *looks relieved: he is not to be assaulted. To* CHARLIE) Your cell is not extra good, but it's better than this Irish pig's pigsty—and you know how to make your bed up. Well, show 'im, and try and get some shape on this bloody lot before the R.C. priest gets 'ere.
   (He goes out. CHARLIE *and* BRENDAN *regard each other happily)*

CHARLIE   This is a bit of all right, Pad, 'n't it?

BRENDAN   Handy enough. That's an awful whore's melt, that screw, Charlie.

CHARLIE *(Starts to make the bed over)* He is and all, china, there's nothing the matter with your furniture, the way it's laid out. *(Nods toward the regulations)*

It's just like it says on the card there—the bedclothes could do with a bit of straightening out. *(BRENDAN helps him arrange the bedding)* But the screws just find fault with everyone. It's like in the Glass'ouse. They give you a toothbrush and an eggcup of soapy water, and tell you to scrub the lawn. It's just to be bastards, that's all. *(Lowers his voice)* The screws don't like Irishmen. According to what he was saying, Pad, they got the dead needle for you, Pad, the screws. *(Worried and embarrassed)* And Pad, some of the blokes don't fancy you, neither.

BRENDAN   They can go hump off, Charlie. I didn't expect anyone to lay down a red carpet for me if I was pinched over here.

CHARLIE   I don't care, Paddy, if you were in the I.R.A. or what you were bleedin' in. You're my china, Paddy.
        (BRENDAN looks into CHARLIE's steadfast, serious eyes, and smiles)

BRENDAN   I know that, Charlie.

CHARLIE *(Smiling back)*   That's straight-up, Pad.
        (SECOND WARDER comes in; he takes in the situation at a glance)

SECOND WARDER *(Stiffly)*   You should be finished now.

CHARLIE   Yes, sir, I was just showin' 'im.

SECOND WARDER   Well, go down to the bagroom, you. We've no married quarters 'ere.

CHARLIE *(Wounded)*   Yes, sir.
        (He goes out quickly without looking up)

SECOND WARDER   You get ready for the R.C. priest.
  (He goes out. BEHAN *comes in to one side)*

BRENDAN   Yes, sir.
  (He kneels beside the bed)

BEHAN   The day I made my First Communion—*(He smiles and shakes his head)*—I prayed to God to take me when I would go straight to heaven. Napoleon did the same. I was a daily communicant sometimes—in spasms—especially during Lent. Then I had difficulties, when I was thirteen or so. With myself and—sex. *(Resentfully)* And with the Catholic Church too, because they always seemed to be against the Republicans. But I never gave up the Faith! Even in this smelly nineteenth-century English lavatory, I made up my mind to pray to Our Lady, the Delight of the Gael, the Pride of Poets and Artists—Dante, François Villon—and maybe out of being here I would get back into the state of grace and stop in it . . . well, not stop out of it.

SECOND WARDER *(Enters; shouts)*   Attention!
  (The CHAPLAIN *appears. He is a stout block of a man, going bald; he is wearing glasses, and when he speaks it is with an English "Haw, old boy" accent.* BRENDAN *takes an eager step toward him)*

BRENDAN *(Smiling respectfully)*   Good evening, Father.

CHAPLAIN *(Unbending; glares)*   When are you going to give up this business? *(*BRENDAN *is taken aback and stares at him in astonishment)* Haven't you any manners, Behan?

SECOND WARDER   Answer Father Lane, Behan.

BRENDAN (*Quietly*) I don't know what business you are talking about, Father.

CHAPLAIN You know perfectly well. Your membership of this murder gang, the I.R.A.

BRENDAN (*Gripping tight*) The I.R.A. is not a murder gang, Father.

SECOND WARDER Don't answer Father Lane back, you f-f-f—
  (*He holds back the expletive with difficulty, up-raising his clenched fist*)

CHAPLAIN (*Waving a restraining hand and sighing*) Mr. Holmes. (*They exchange sympathetic nods; he starts up again patiently*) Cardinal Hinsley and the bishops of England have issued pastorals denouncing the I.R.A., and while you're here I can *not* let you come to the altar, unless you tell me once and for all that you will have nothing more to do with this gang.
  (*He regards* BRENDAN *with narrow eyes, his lips tight with authority*)

BRENDAN (*With an effort to keep a steady voice*) Why should the bishops of England have the right to dictate about politics to an Irishman, Father?

CHAPLAIN The bishops of Ireland have denounced the I.R.A., Behan, time and again, even early this year. The Church has always been Ireland's best friend— in Ireland, here in England, and all over the world. I must inform you that your own clergy and hierarchy have excommunicated the I.R.A. (*At this,* BRENDAN *opens his mouth to reply, but the* CHAPLAIN *restrains him with upraised hand*) You are *automatically* ex-

35

communicated unless you repent of your sin in being a member of it, and promise God in confession to sever all connection with it. *(Changing his tone to one of sweet reason)* Surely you can't set yourself up against the bishops? You, an ignorant lad, against educated men who have spent their lifetime studying these matters?

BRENDAN *(Fiercely)* I didn't spend a lifetime studying theology, but I know that the Church has always been against Ireland and for the British Empire.

BEHAN You could sing that if you had an air to it.

BRENDAN With no disrespect for you, Father, a synod of Irish bishops eight hundred years ago decided to excommunicate any Irishman who refused to acknowledge the King of England as his ruler. That was only three years after the Normans landed, and held only a bit of the country. Even after the Reformation, the O'Neills in Ulster had to threaten the Pope that they would burn the Catholic archbishop out of the cathedral if he didn't take Queen Elizabeth's soldiers out of it.

   (He is gathering steam)

BEHAN What about 1798?

BRENDAN In 1798, weren't the rebels excommunicated and wasn't Father John Murphy, that was burned alive by the English yeomen, excommunicated?

SECOND WARDER Look here, you—
   (The CHAPLAIN has dropped his tolerant look for one of surprised anger)

BRENDAN And during the famine didn't they tell the people to give up their crops and die of the hunger in the ditches at home, with the grass-juice running green from the dead mouth of a mother clutching a live infant?

CHAPLAIN (*Roars*) Here, you—!

BRENDAN Weren't all the Irish patriots excommunicated, and didn't the bishop of Cork excommunicate the I.R.A. and support the Black and Tans? Wasn't— (*The priest backs to the door*)—wasn't my own *father* excommunicated? (*Calls after the exiting* CHAPLAIN) So feck off, you fat bastard! And to hell with England, and to hell with Rome! Up the Republic!

SECOND WARDER (*Shouts*) You swine! (*Hits* BRENDAN *on the back of his neck*) Mr. Whitbread! Mr. Whitbread, sir! (FIRST WARDER *enters, on the run.* SECOND WARDER *is almost gasping with indignation. He has a half-nelson on* BRENDAN) This—Irish swine—insulting—the priest—

FIRST WARDER (*Through gritted teeth*) You fecking shit-'ouse, we'll teach you how to be'ave. (*He beats* BRENDAN, *who goes down sprawling. They kick him; become breathless with exertion*) Filthy swine. Insulting—the—priest! Irish bastard!

  (FIRST WARDER *goes out. The cell is in disorder from the fray—bedclothes scattered, bedboards and furniture overturned.* BRENDAN *cowers in a ball to protect himself*)

SECOND WARDER Get up, you pig! Clean up this bloody mess. Get this pigsty straightened out!

(He deliberately overturns the chair, then goes out, slamming the cell door and locking it)

BEHAN Maybe this will cure you of the idea that religion of any description has anything to do with mercy or pity or love. And when they come to you with their creeping Jesus gab, you'll say to them, "What about the night in Walton Jail?"

BRENDAN Me mouth is raw and bleedin' . . . an', God, me kidneys are sore. If that's the things you have on your sides.

(He lies down on the bed)

BEHAN Ah, well! Maybe this bit of a belting I got would be a contributory cause of an early death in the years to come . . . but, sure, what matter of that?

(He exits. For the first few moments, BRENDAN does not stir. He is gasping for breath. A key is heard in the door. He starts in terror. The cell door opens. BROWNY comes in, carrying two books. With him is the LIBRARY WARDER. BRENDAN gazes at them, dazed and uncomprehending. BROWNY sets the two books on the table, after righting it. The LIBRARY WARDER has a pencil poised over a pad and glances up at BROWNY, who calls out the titles)

BROWNY Three-five-oh-one, Behan. Fiction: *Under the Greenwood Tree*, Hardy . . . Nonfiction: *Selfridge's Furniture Catalogue.*

LIBRARY WARDER *(As he writes, and with an easygoing cockney accent)* Don't go swopping them, now, you

—unless you want to 'ave a little trip down to chokey.*

(BROWNY *hastily rights the rest of the furniture, smiling at* BRENDAN)

BRENDAN (*Fervently*)   I will not, sir, and thanks very much.

LIBRARY WARDER   Don't thank me, thank the Lord. You're an Irishman, ain't you? Ever 'ear of the great Irish leader, Michael Collins?

BRENDAN   Michael Collins gave my mother a five-pound note on O'Connell Bridge a few months before I was born, when my father was locked up by Michael Collins' Government.

LIBRARY WARDER (*Looks toward ceiling, searching his memory*)   I got a book about Ireland. Remind me about it or ask for it by writing on your slate for me when we come round Tuesday next week. Write on it: "Please leave the Irish book! *The Faerie Queene*."

BROWNY   P'raps 'e don't like dirty books!

BRENDAN (*Softly, looking gratefully from the warder to* BROWNY)   Thank you very much, and I'll leave you the note if I don't see you.

LIBRARY WARDER (*At the cell door*)   Right, Paddy.

BROWNY (*Smiling*)   It'll be all right, Paddy. My name's Browny.

(*He goes out. The* LIBRARY WARDER *pauses at the*

* Solitary confinement.

door, turns back to BRENDAN *with a grin and gives
a thumbs-up gesture)*

LIBRARY WARDER *(Sotto voce)* Up the Republic!
(He exits, locking the door. BRENDAN *stands open-
mouthed at the mystery of the world. He stares
after the warder, wiping his bloody nose on his
sleeve)*

BRENDAN   It's a queer world, God knows, but the best
we have to be going on with.
*(He lies down on the bed. The prisoners troop
in, collect their mailbags and commence to stitch,
sitting in various places on the stage.* BROWNY
*sits at a table, checking a list. Somewhere a
prisoner is making a noise of bagpipes)*

FIRST WARDER *(Through his teeth)* 'Oo's making that
bleedin' noise, eh? *(The prisoners open their mouths
so the warder can see they are not making the noise.
He stares intently at each face in turn, in a quiet
frenzy, but still the piping goes on. The piping ceases.
He starts back to his place. The piping resumes,
resolute though quiet. He stares about him, cocks his
head to see if he is imagining the noise, then nods
slowly. The warder fixes his eyes on one prisoner,
dives through the ranks, collars* JOCK) It's you, you
Scotch bastard. Want to play your bleedin' bagpipes,
do you? Mr. 'Olmes, sir!

JOCK   W-wait, sir . . . I . . . It wasn't me. I swear it
wasn't . . .

FIRST WARDER   Playing the bleedin' bagpipes through
'is bleedin' teeth, 'e was. (SECOND WARDER *enters, takes*

JOCK *by the scruff of the neck, drags him off. They hear a new sound; this time it is whistling. The warder looks down stupidly on them. He goes through the same routine again. He comes to* DALE *and* CALLAN. DALE *indicates* CALLAN) Callan! So it's you—Irish scum!

(*He pounces on* CALLAN)

CALLAN Up the Republic!

FIRST WARDER We'll give you "Up the Republic!" You swine!
(*The warders drag him off;* DALE *leaps up and darts to the table;* JAMES *follows*)

DALE Finished work. (*Puts his bag down. He grabs* BROWNY *and throws him to* JAMES) You were down to the loo, wa'nt you?

BROWNY (*Terrified*) 'Ere, what's eating you, tosh?

DALE You know bloody well what's eating me. Where's me fag-ends?

BROWNY What?

DALE (*Snarling*) Me fecking fag-ends that you knocked off, 'at's what.

BROWNY I didn't, tosh—honest to Christ, I didn't. Swear to—

TUBBY Nick, nick!
(DALE *hears* FIRST WARDER *approaching and runs back with his bag*)

FIRST WARDER   Silence!

DALE *(Holding his bag aloft)*   Finished work.

FIRST WARDER   Right. And remember, four stitches to the inch, all neat and proper-like, or you'll be needing a few stitches yourselves.
> *(The prisoners begin to sew quietly. The warder saunters away, and as soon as his back is turned, the prisoners behave like schoolboys, whispering behind their hands, signaling each other, laughing silently.* DALE *nudges* JAMES *again, and then leans toward* BRENDAN *on his other side)*

DALE *(To* BRENDAN*)*   Irishman, eh, Paddy?

BRENDAN   I am.

DALE   My mum was Irish, Paddy. *(*BRENDAN *sews on, noncommittal)* But that don't mean I like Paddies. Bleedin' scabs, the Paddies. Come over to Liverpool and work for scab wages.

BRENDAN *(Offended)*   Irishmen are not scabs—

JAMES   Why don't you all stay 'ome in starvin' Ireland?

DALE   With the pigs in the parlor, instead of scabbing on honest blokes.

BRENDAN *(Flaring up)*   Y-y-you're wr-wr-wrong. We m-make good wages in Ireland. We—
> *(*DALE *turns on* BRENDAN *as though* BRENDAN *has done something to him, and as though he is just barely restraining himself from giving him a belt)*

DALE *(So that the warder will hear)* Shag off, you Killarney mick, or I'll 'it you.

FIRST WARDER *(Angrily)* What's to-do down there?

DALE It's this Irish mick, sir. 'E keeps talking all the time. I just told 'im 'e'd get me in trouble.

BRENDAN That's a bloody lie. H-h-he . . . s-s-spoke t-t-to m-me f-first!

FIRST WARDER *(Boring in venomously)* I'm just about browned off with you. Move over there—(BRENDAN *starts to object)*—and shut your hole. Move over there. Get on with it, I shan't warn you again, I shan't. I've warned you before.

BROWNY Can I go to the loo, sir?

FIRST WARDER *(Moving away)* What, again? What you want is a bottle of gin for your kidneys. Oh, all right. Dale, you take over from Brown.
(BROWNY *gets up and leaves.* DALE *jumps up)*

DALE Yes, sir.
(He glances at JAMES*)*

FIRST WARDER Right, James, you help Dale.

JAMES Thank you, sir.
(They go behind the table and begin fussing with the bags and supplies)

CHARLIE Finished work, sir.
(He holds up his bag. The warder nods assent.

43

CHARLIE *takes his bag to the table.* DALE *gives it a cursory inspection and hands it to* JAMES. JAMES *gives* CHARLIE *a replacement to work on.* CHARLIE *returns to his seat. The warder paces offstage and back)*

BRENDAN *(Holding his bag up)* Finished, sir. *(The warder nods.* BRENDAN *gets up.* DALE *nudges* JAMES *and they smirk as* BRENDAN *goes to the table. To* DALE*)* Finished work.
*(*DALE *grabs the bag rudely and makes a thing of inspecting it. He assumes a pained expression)*

DALE   Mr. Whitbread, sir?
(He holds out the bag for the warder to see. FIRST WARDER *looks at it quickly and thrusts it back at* BRENDAN*)*

FIRST WARDER   You stupid Irish mick. Four to the inch, four to the inch. Now pick it up and do it proper.
*(*DALE *and* JAMES *laugh.* BRENDAN *looks at* DALE, *then at* JAMES. *He goes back to his chair, sits down and rips some stitches and starts sewing again.* CHARLIE *throws furtive and worried glances at him)*

DALE *(Not loud enough to carry to the warder)*   Stupid Irish mick!

JAMES   'Ow's the pigs in the parlor, Paddy?
(They all get convulsed)

DALE   Leave 'im alone, can't you see 'e's 'omesick? 'E misses the pigs and prayties.
(There are more snickers)

44

HARTY   Finished work.

FIRST WARDER   Right.
> (*They all bend over their work.* CHARLIE *nudges* BRENDAN, *and taking* BRENDAN's *bag, gives him his own, nodding toward the table.* BRENDAN *holds it aloft*)

BRENDAN   Finished work. (*He barely waits for the warder's nod. He fingers the metal palm on his hand, then strides up to the table and stands there till* JAMES *stands up.* BRENDAN *holds out the bag to him*) That's finished work!

JAMES (*With a thick sneer*)   Oh, is it? (*He looks at it in great annoyance—glad, though, to have another diversion at* BRENDAN's *expense. He looks at* BRENDAN *and takes up the bag. All the others watch intently*) What's to do with you? That's another you 'aven't done right. 'Ere, take it back and do it again, cop.
> (*He flings the bag at* BRENDAN. DALE *laughs.* BRENDAN *knocks* JAMES *down, and thrashes him with his metal thimble.* FIRST WARDER *rushes in and breaks up the fight. Blood is pouring from* JAMES' *face*)

FIRST WARDER   Mr. 'Olmes!
> (*The* SECOND WARDER *comes on the run*)

SECOND WARDER   What is it, sir?

FIRST WARDER   Been a bit of a bother 'ere. You take James to the hospital while I take Behan before the Governor.

SECOND WARDER (*To* JAMES) Right, come on, take your 'and off your eyes if you don't want to trip over yourself and do yourself some more damage. You are a bloody mess.

> (*He leads the moaning* JAMES *off. The* FIRST WARDER *turns back to* BRENDAN *and takes him by the arm. There is no laughing or grinning or leering or jibing in the prisoners now. They look at* BRENDAN, *and he, head high, looks down on them in triumph.* CHARLIE *gives him a proud and friendly look. The prisoners troop off, taking chairs with them. Elderly* PRISON GOVERNOR *comes in and sits behind the table.* BRENDAN *is marched around to face him*)

FIRST WARDER Stand to the mat and state your full name, number, age, religion and sentence.

BRENDAN Behan, Brendan, sir. Three-five-oh-one, age sixteen, Roman Catholic, awaiting trial.

PRISON GOVERNOR We'll win—er—we'll win all the time. We can make it—er—very bad for you—er—it's all the same to us. And it's up to you—er—whatever way you want it.

BRENDAN Yes, sir.

> (*The governor reads the papers given to him by the warder. Now* BEHAN *comes in to one side of the stage*)

BEHAN Yes, sir, said I, with my hands at the seams of my trousers and looking manly, admitting my fault to this tired old consul, weary from his labors amongst the lesser breeds, administering the King's justice equal and fairly to wild Irish and turbulent Pathan, teaching fair play to the wily Arab and a sense of sportsmanship to the smooth Confucian. In my ballocks, said I, you dull scruffy old creeping Jesus, gone past the Bengal Lancer act now. Any decent horse would drop dead from the shame if you managed to get up on its back.

PRISON GOVERNOR   I must take this opportunity of warning you that if this assault had been carried out on one of my officers, you would most certainly have been flogged. I sentence you to one day's cellular confinement, one day's deprivation of mattress, and one day's Number One diet.
      (*He exits, stiff and bowlegged*)

BEHAN   Yoicks! Tallyho!

FIRST WARDER (*Roars*)   Attention! About turn! March! (BRENDAN *is marched around to the door of his cell, which is now stripped of bedclothes, etc.*) Now take off your stockings, your shoes and your jacket, and put them outside here.
      (BRENDAN *strips, gathers his clothes in a bundle, starts to hand them to* FIRST WARDER, *then realizes his blunder*)

BRENDAN   It's very cold, isn't it, sir?

FIRST WARDER   Never mind about the weather. I'll give you a kick that will send your ass up to your shoulder blades.
      (BRENDAN *puts his clothes outside the cell, and comes back in*)

BRENDAN (*As the warder leaves*)   Thank you, sir. (*The warder slams the cell door, locks it and goes off.*

47

BRENDAN *shudders with the cold, blows on his hands to warm them, and takes out a bucket to sit on. A book falls out of it. Looking at the title)* Cranford, by Mrs. Gaskell. Jaysus! *(He puts the book under his arm and begins to whistle softly, pacing his cell. Warders are heard shouting distantly. He stops)* I'd sing out loud, only they might hear me.

BEHAN Better to be defiant in a quiet sort of way. These sportsmen would be serious men if it came to kicking the shit out of you. A terrible thing for the Germans or the Russians or the Fuzzie-Wuzzies to do as much to one of theirs, and a crime against humanity. *(Shrugs)* Still, you can't blame them. Everyone has his own way of looking at things.

BRENDAN *(Sniffs)* I can smell the dinner. *(He whistles a few furious bars)* That it may choke you, you shower of bastards!

BEHAN Think of Terence MacSwiney, lad—longest hunger strike on record: seventy-eight days with no scoff at all.

BRENDAN And me father, on hunger strike with thousands of others.

BEHAN Didn't MacSwiney drive the bastards mad with the publicity he was getting? They were up and offering him every conceivable delicacy: chicken, ham, turkey, roast pork, steak—

BRENDAN Oh, for the love of Jaysus, give over. Mother of Christ, aren't there a thousand places between Belfast and Bantry Bay where a fellow would be stuffed with grub, not to mind dowsed with porter, if he could only be there and here at the same time?

BEHAN   I suppose that would be like trying to get a drink at your own funeral. (DALE *starts across the stage, sees* BROWNY *and* FIRST WARDER *coming from the other side, passes them and goes out.* BEHAN *acts the host*) Make way there, you with the face, and let in the man that's doing jail for Ireland, and suffering hunger and abuse amongst that parcel of white-livered—

BRENDAN   —thin-lipped—

BEHAN   —paper-waving—

BRENDAN   —key-rattling hangmen over—
         (*He spins around. The warder opens up the cell to let* BROWNY *in; goes off*)

BROWNY   'Ello. 'Ere, Paddy, lad, I 'ave your cob and water. (*Soft and smiling*) It's not much but it'll keep the guts together till teatime.

BRENDAN (*Taking the can of water and bread*)   Do I get more then?

BROWNY   'Course you do. And more tomorrow. You're out then at dinnertime and all's well again.

BRENDAN   But I thought it was three days—

BROWNY   Nay, you silly feller, 'tis all one day.

BRENDAN   Well, it was worth it, to give that bastard James a trimming.

BROWNY *(Worried)* Only thing to be afeered of is 'im or 'is china, Dale, coming at you all of a sudden.

BRENDAN I'll look out for that, Browny.

BROWNY Bit of snout, Pad?

BRENDAN Thanks, Browny.

BROWNY And 'ere's match.

BRENDAN Your blood should be bottled.

BROWNY Don't thank me, Pad. Thank Dale. *(He glances over his shoulder to make sure he is unheard, then grins)* Screw, 'e empties bucket of butts down loo. Some float 'round, like. Dale, 'e fishes butts out, puts on sill to dry. I nip in and knock them off.
> *(BRENDAN looks down at the butt and then holds it up to BROWNY)*

BRENDAN Was that down the loo? Big daddy Dale's? Jaysus!
> *(BROWNY nods, BRENDAN sniffs the butt and they both laugh)*

BROWNY Lots more where that came from. Be back in a minute.
> *(He smiles and winks and goes off. BRENDAN protests)*

BEHAN John Howard, the Quaker, invented solitary, they say. He must have had terrible little to do. These religious maniacs, they have empty minds on account of not going in for sex or sports or drink, or swim-

ming or reading bad books. And Satan will find work
for idle hands.
(He goes out)

DALE *(Offstage)* Browny, I've got you, you little bastard.

BROWNY *(Offstage)* No, no, Dale, I was only kidding ...
(Screams are heard. BROWNY *comes in, lurching
crazily, clutching his wounds and trying to hold
himself up. He totters and collapses.* BRENDAN
comes out of his cell quickly and runs to BROWNY)

BRENDAN Oh, Jaysus!

FIRST WARDER *(Running in)* You know anything about
this, Behan?

BRENDAN No, sir.

FIRST WARDER We'll see about that. Better get 'im to
'ospital.
*(*SECOND WARDER *rushes in)*

SECOND WARDER What's to do? What happened to
Brown?

FIRST WARDER Got 'imself carved up. 'E's passed out.
Get back to your cell, Behan.
(Both warders pick up BROWNY *and drag him off)*

BRENDAN Yes, sir.
*(*CHARLIE *and* CALLAN *have entered, carrying buckets of water and mops)*

CHARLIE All for a miserable bit of snout. Poor Browny.

CALLAN The screws know Dale did it, anyway—cut him into ribbons with a razor. I hope they kick 'im 'round a bit, the perishing bastard.
(*The* FIRST WARDER *returns*)

FIRST WARDER Behan, I told you to get back in your cell! (BRENDAN *goes back and gets locked in. He looks down at the floor*) Christ, what a mess. Millwall—

CHARLIE Yes, sir.

FIRST WARDER Bring your bucket over here. Be'aving like a pack of dirty animals. All right, get on with it. It's this sort of thing that turns a good officer wicked.
(*He leaves.* CHARLIE *goes to the cell and hands* BRENDAN *a cigarette through the peephole*)

CHARLIE Hey, Paddy, it's Charlie. Here's a bit of snout.

BRENDAN Thanks, china.

CALLAN (*Comes over to* BRENDAN'*s peephole*) Behan!

BRENDAN Hello, Callan.

CALLAN Have you heard the news?

BRENDAN About Browny?

CALLAN No, not him—the two I.R.A. men in Birmingham. They're going to hang them tomorrow.

BRENDAN (*Crossing himself*) Tomorrow. Ash Wednesday.

CALLAN (*Fiercely*) Two innocent men.

BRENDAN   Don't we all know that.

CALLAN *(First looking up and down the landing)*   Here. *(He takes a newspaper from under his shirt and pushes it in to* BRENDAN*)* Read it yourself.

BRENDAN   "Before he was sentenced to death, one of the I.R.A. prisoners told the court that he would walk out smiling, thinking of all the other men that had died for Ireland. The judge said, 'May the Lord have mercy on your soul' and the condemned replied, 'You, too.'" It says here that there are demonstrations by the Irish all over America.

CALLAN   And there'll be one here tonight, too!

BRENDAN *(Dumbfounded)*   Here?

CALLAN   My cell is right above yours. I'll signal on the pipes.
   (He goes off)

BRENDAN   Callan! I wouldn't try that here . . . *(Getting frantic)* Callan! It's a truce I want, not a bloody demonstration. Do you want to be kicked to death or insanity? *(He paces the cell in agitation)* Yes, because they're even bigger bastards and crueler bastards than I ever took them for. Jaysus, aren't my kidneys still paining me from the beating they gave me. *(He rushes back to the peephole)* Callan, you bloody madman! Not here, not here, for dear Jaysus' sake—*not here!* *(He runs his hands through his hair)* That's it—a read. I'll have a read. *(He takes the book, then looks up with a sudden thought)* Maybe Callan would keep easy till morning. *(Reads)* "For Miss Barker had ordered all sorts of good things for supper—scalloped oysters, potted lobster—(CALLAN *enters far upstage and begins tapping on the floor with a bucket.* BRENDAN *starts nervously, and turns his head slowly and apprehensively in the direction of the tapping. It stops, then starts again, louder. He goes back to his book)*—potted lobster, jelly, a dish called 'Little Cupids'—*(There is more tapping)*—macaroons sopped in brandy, I should have called it, if I had not known its more refined classical name. In short we were to—(CALLAN *taps again)*—to be feasted."

CALLAN *(Roaring unmercifully)* Uuuuuup the Re-puuuublic!

BRENDAN *(Springs up wildly from the mattress; furious sotto voce)* That the devil may choke you and the Republic!
    (He cocks his head and listens grimly)

CALLAN Be-eee-han. Bren-daaaaaan Be-eehaaaaaaan!

BRENDAN *(Goes mad; still sotto voce)* You louse-bound bastard. Don't drag me into it! You're not much good alone and unarmed, are you? Leave me out of it!

CALLAN Uuuuuuuup the Rep-uuuuuuub-lic!

BRENDAN Holy Mother of God! Give the man back his overcoat and leave the Republic to look after itself.

CALLAN Be-eeeeeee-han! Get up and give a shout—a sh-ooooooooooouuuuuuuut!

BRENDAN *(Franticly and low)* A kick in the ass is what

I'd like to give you. *(He stands for a moment, wondering what to do)* May God direct me!

CALLAN   Uuuuuuuu-uuu-uuup the Rep-uuub-lic, Beee-haaan!

BRENDAN   All right. All right. *(He goes to the vent above the pipes, puts his mouth to it, and shouts discreetly down)* Up the Republic! *(He looks over his shoulder fearfully)*

CALLAN   I caaaaaaaaa-an't heeeear youuuuuuu riiiightly.

BRENDAN *(Into the vent)*   I'm shouting. The walls here are three feet thick.

CALLAN   All right. Goooood maaaaan. Up the Reeeee-puuuuub-lic!

BRENDAN *(Even lower)*   Up the Republic. We defy you. To hell with the British Empire.
> *(There is a brouhaha of voices; the jangling of keys is heard from below.* BRENDAN *jumps back onto his mattress, and feigns concentration in his book. The warders run up to his cell door, and open it)*

SECOND WARDER   What are you doing there, Behan?
> *(*BRENDAN *puts down his book innocently)*

BRENDAN   I'm reading, sir. *(The warders close the door and go off. They reenter upstage to where* CALLAN *is, and drag him off as he yells and curses)* They've taken him to chokey! *(Reads)* " 'It's very strong,' said Miss Pole as she put down her empty glass. 'I do be-

lieve there's spirit in it. I often feel tipsy myself from eating damson tart,' said Miss Barker." *(He listens)* Up the Republic . . .
> *(It is a whisper only. Darkness)*

BEHAN *(Enters and sings)*
> Let cowards mock and tyrants frown,
> Ah, little do we care.
> A felon's cap is the noblest crown
> An Irish head can wear.
> And, brothers, say, shall we today
> Unmoved, like cowards stand,
> While traitors shame and foes defame
> The felons of our land.
>> *(The stage is cleared of the cells. A crowd comes in, as if to court.* BRENDAN *stands in the center, looking out toward the audience)*

VOICE OF CLERK   His Majesty versus Elsie Jankins, Elsie Jankins, Elsie Jankins. His Majesty versus Brendan Behan, Brendan Behan, Brendan Behan.

VOICE OF JUDGE   Is the prisoner represented?

BEHAN   I'll represent him, Your Honor, seein' there's no one else. *(Aside, to* BRENDAN*)* Refuse to recognize the court.

BRENDAN   As a soldier of the Irish Republican Army, I refuse to recognize the court.

BEHAN   Sure, he's only a foolish boy that never stood a chance, Your Honor. Connected with the I.R.A. since he could walk. Didn't he see his father for the first time through the bars of a prison?

VOICE OF JUDGE   The court—

BEHAN   A-a-a-ah, don't be too hard on him now, and
he'll give his word not to attend any more parades,
and drop out of the I.R.A., and attend more to his
trade, and go out dancing or something and—and—
and get married. (*To* BRENDAN) Won't you, you
*amadan?**

BRENDAN   The young Irish hero, Cuchulainn, with his
enemies ringed 'round him, held his back to a tree
and called on the gods of death and grandeur to hold
him up till his last blood flowed.

BEHAN   Last blood? Sure to God, you'll kill yourself
more with the drink than you ever will with the I.R.A.

VOICE OF JUDGE   The court finds the prisoner mute of
malice. Enter a plea of "Not Guilty." Has the prisoner anything to say before sentence is passed?

BEHAN   Has he? He's been workin' on the bloody
speech for a month. (*To* BRENDAN) Go on, and mind
the oul' stutter!

BRENDAN   My lord and gentlemen, it is my privilege
and honor today to stand, as so many of my countrymen have done—

VOICE OF JUDGE   Neither the jury nor this court wish to
listen to a political speech.

BRENDAN   —as so many of my countrymen have done, in
an English court, to testify to the unyielding deter-

* Stupid person.

mination of the Irish people to regain every inch
of our national territory and to give expression to
the noble aspirations for which so much Irish blood
has been shed, so many brave and manly hearts have
been broken, and for which so many of my comrades
are now lying in your jails . . .

BEHAN Go on, now—throw the hammer after the
hatchet!

BRENDAN . . . and this . . . and this to a proud and in-
telligent people, who had a language, a literature,
when the barbarian woad-painted Briton was first
learning to walk upright. By plantation, famine, and
massacre, you have striven to drive the people of
Ireland from off the soil of Ireland, but in seven
centuries you have not succeeded, and until the thirty-
two-county Republic of Ireland is once more func-
tioning, Ireland unfree shall never be at peace.

BEHAN No surrender!

VOICE OF JUDGE *(In a temper)* Prisoner at the bar, you
have taken advantage of the mildness of British law
in regard to the punishment of persons under eighteen.

BEHAN I'll tell you what your man the judge is going
to say now. He's going to say that in this court, you'll
get justice the like of which you'll get nowhere else
in the world. Which is what the judge told the two
I.R.A. men in Birmingham. And then he sentenced
them to be hanged. Which they were.

(BRENDAN *remains silent*)

VOICE OF JUDGE   This court regrets that it cannot sentence you to the fourteen years penal servitude you so richly deserve.

BEHAN   Thanks be to Jaysus!

VOICE OF JUDGE   Though young in age, you are mature in purpose—

BEHAN   Oh, indeed!

VOICE OF JUDGE   —and I deeply regret that the law makes no allowance for persons of your type. I now sentence you to three years' Borstal detention.

BEHAN and BRENDAN (*Shouting together*)   Up the Republic!

   (BRENDAN *is led away by a policeman and a sergeant*)

BEHAN (*Sings*)

> Some in the convict's dreary cell,
> Have found a living tomb,
> And some unseen, unfriended, fell
> Within the dungeon's gloom,
> But what care we, although it be
> Trod by a ruffian band,
> God bless the clay where rest today
> The felons of our land . . .

Curtain

ACT TWO

The scene is Hollesley Bay, a boys' Borstal on the eastern coast of England. As the curtain rises, the BORSTAL BOYS *are sitting on stools, as if on a moving bus.* BEHAN *is singing.*

BEHAN

> There was burglars and ponces and forgers,
> Rapers and robbers and homicides, too,
> There was thieves, pickpockets, shoplifters,
> In the Hollesley Bay criminal zoo,
> There was murderers there in abundance,
> 'Twould make old Bluebeard turn pale,
> 'Twould kill a lad twice, to be travelin' so nice,
> On the bus to the Hollesley Bay jail.

WELSH WARDER *(Enters; blows a whistle)* All out! *(Bellows)* Answer when your name is called! *(*BEHAN *has now nonchalantly seated himself at the side of the stage, where he comments on the boys)* Five-two-nine, Hartigan.

HARTY 'Ere, sir.

BEHAN He's in for screwing. Not in the dictionary. Means lifting, fecking, removing or otherwise converting for own use.

63

HARTY   I been screwing since I was ten. I 'ad to. I wouldn't 'ave eaten if I didn't. *(Plucks his shorts)* This is like the bleedin' Boy Scouts.

WELSH WARDER   Five-three-oh, Da Vinci.

JOE   'Ere, sir.

BEHAN   Piccadilly pimp.

JOE   I'm out of my natural element. I feel like a fecking whore at a christening.

WELSH WARDER   Five-three-one, Jones.

KEN   Here, sir.

BEHAN   H.M.P. His Majesty's Pleasure. That means murder.

KEN   I've a brother who'll spring me from this place, just wait and see.

WELSH WARDER   Five-three-two, Tonks.

CHEWLIPS   'Ere, sir.

BEHAN   Chewlips. Yeh, that's what we call him, Chewlips, because he pinched a truckload of tulips.

CHEWLIPS   Fruit and flowers, that's my trade. *(Bawls)* Foh-pance a pahnd—pehhs!*

BORSTAL BOYS   Shut up, can't you.

* Four pence a pound—pears!

64

BEHAN He's not as green as he looks. Has the stuff stashed away somewhere.

WELSH WARDER Five-three-three, Smith.

JOCK Here, sir.

BEHAN Jock. Rape.

JOCK It were all a mistake.

BEHAN The course of true love never runs smooth.

JOCK Never trust a judy.

BEHAN *(Winks)* Could happen to a fellow with his own girl.

JOCK It did.

WELSH WARDER Five-three-four, Millwall.

CHARLIE 'Ere, sir.

BEHAN Good old Charlie.

CHARLIE Up the Hoy Har Hay!

BEHAN The English are the worst.

WELSH WARDER Five-three-five, Meadows.

TOM 'Ere, sir. *(With loathing)* Fine lot! Thieves, pimps, rapists. They're just a dirty, degenerate scum, and no decent lad should have ought to do with them.

BEHAN   Thanks be to God he's not on the bench at the
Old Bailey. It'd be a poor day for the prisoners in the
dock if he was.

WELSH WARDER   Five-three-six, Rivers.

RIVERS   Here, sir.

BEHAN   Cat burglar. Oxford.

RIVERS   No, no, no—Harrow.

BEHAN   Likes it better here, though.

RIVERS   The grub's much better.

BOYS   Good show!

RIVERS   Bloody good show.

WELSH WARDER   Five-three-seven, Cragg.

CRAGG   Here, sir.

BEHAN   Decent bloke. He thinks the world is flat.

CRAGG   It's not altogether flat. There's bumps here and
there for mountains and such like. But mostly it's flat.

BEHAN   Another H.M.P. Domestic problems.

CRAGG   A little difference of opinion with me late
father-in-law.

WELSH WARDER   Five-three-eight, Callaghan.

66

SHAGGY 'Ere, sir.

BEHAN Shaggy. Ex-British Army, believe it or not. Caught selling his rifle to the I.R.A.

SHAGGY I was stationed in Northern Ireland, at Bally-kinlar.

BEHAN The Belfast I.R.A. got so many rifles from Ballykinlar, they used to call it the Stores.

WELSH WARDER Five-three-nine, Bee-haun.

BRENDAN Still here, sir.

WELSH WARDER Don't you try any smart answers with me, Bee-han, or I shall clip your bloody ear'ole.

BORSTAL BOYS *(In chorus)* Runnin' round with bleedin' time bombs.

WELSH WARDER 'Ere, I seem to 'ave one too many. 'Ave you sods been breeding? *(Counts again)* Right. That's it, then. Grub's up!
   (He blows his whistle. The boys break up and re-form, as if at a table. The warder leaves)

JOE Smashin' scoff!

CHEWLIPS *(Happily)* Foh-pance a pahnd—pehhs!

BORSTAL BOYS Cor! Stuff it, will you?

HARTY Smashin' scoff? Bloody sickening, I calls it. Can't

keep it on me stomach. Too much, all of a sudden.
(He tears offstage)

CRAGG   There's always a certain amount of diarrhea among new blokes.

JOE   'Course, there's some blokes couldn't be 'appy no matter where they were. If they was in the Ritz 'Otel with a million nicker and Rita 'Ayworth they'd still find some bloody thing to moan about.

RIVERS *(To CHEWLIPS)*   What exactly are you doing?

CHEWLIPS *(Abashed)*   Fixin' me 'air s'all!

JOE   With margarine? 'E's puttin' the margarine on 'is 'air!
(HARTY reenters)

SHAGGY *(To BRENDAN)*   What did they cop you for, Paddy?

CHARLIE   'E's political.

HARTY   Tried to blow up Cammell Lairds Shipyards, 'e did.

RIVERS   How about the poor blighters working there, and their wives and kids?

JOE   Why didn't you do in some of the big pots?

CHEWLIPS   Like that old Lady Astor.

JOE   Instead of puttin' bombs in railway stations.

HARTY   Bloody lot of murderers. What about—

CHARLIE   'Ere, let 'im alone. Turn it up, can't you?

SHAGGY   Oh, kip in, you Croydon puff.

CHARLIE *(Jumping up)*   I won't kip in, you little short-arsed bastard.

BEHAN   Compliments pass when the quality meet.
      (SHAGGY *takes a fighter stance; goes for* CHARLIE)

BRENDAN *(Shouts)*   Leave him alone, you!

SHAGGY   Oh, so you want to bundle, Paddy?

BORSTAL BOYS   Go on! 'Ave a go! Your muvver won't know!

CRAGG *(Like a referee)*   Now, no knee and nut stuff and no catching by the cobs. And break quickly if we give the nick.
      (BRENDAN *and* SHAGGY *circle each other warily*)

BORSTAL BOYS   Give 'im one, Shaggy!

CHARLIE   'E won't, you know.

CRAGG   Come on, get cracking!

HARTY   Like a pair of old judies.

JOE   Go on, less natter and more batter!

(BRENDAN *makes a determined rush at* SHAGGY, *and goes down before a lightning punch.* SHAGGY *stands over him, laughing*)

JOCK (*Raising* SHAGGY's *arm*)   And still champeen!

SHAGGY   Get up, you silly old sod, I could 'ave booted the 'ead off you. (BRENDAN *picks himself up, dazed*) Come on, you silly old silly.

JOE   Just like when you topped the bill at Lambeth Baths, eh, Shaggy?
(BRENDAN *looks from* JOE *to* SHAGGY, *astonished*)

JOCK (*Shadowboxing*)   You didn't know about Shaggy being fly-weight champion of the Army.

SHAGGY   You, being an Irishman, thought you'd 'ave a go at a professional boxer.
(BRENDAN *nods deprecatingly and smiles.* SHAGGY *gives him a cigarette and they all light up*)

CRAGG   Nothing an Irishman likes better than a bundle.

CHEWLIPS   I 'eard my old man say that the Irish will fight till there's only one left—and 'e'll bleedin' well commit suicide 'cause there's no other fecker left to fight with.

WELSH WARDER (*Enters; blows his whistle*)   The Governor!
(*The boys duck their cigarettes. The* GOVERNOR *comes in wearing plus fours. He smiles at them all and nods*)

GOVERNOR (*Very civilly*)   You may sit down.

WELSH WARDER   Sit down!

GOVERNOR   You may smoke. (*They are delighted*) While
you are here, the first thing I ask of you is courtesy
to each other . . .

CHEWLIPS   'Ear that? You've got to be courteous to me.

CHARLIE (*To* CHEWLIPS)   You all right, love?

WELSH WARDER   Silence!

GOVERNOR   Courtesy to the staff and to myself. And in
other matters I must have your cooperation.

BORSTAL BOYS   Yes, sir.

GOVERNOR   We have a great deal to do in the gardens,
on the farm, and keeping the sea back—or we won't
have either. So don't worry, we'll find jobs for you.
(*The boys groan*) Eh, good morning and good luck
to you.
       (*He goes off. The warder exits. The Protestant
       minister comes on*)

MINISTER   Good morning, boys. Welcome to Hollesley
Bay.

BORSTAL BOYS   Good morning.

BRENDAN   Good morning, Father.

MINISTER   Good morning! And God bless you, Paddy,
whoever you are.
       (*He goes off*)

JOE   You shouldn't 'ave called 'im "Father."

BRENDAN   Well, I couldn't have called him "Mother."

CHARLIE   He's the minister. The Church of England bloke.

JOE   'E's not the priest.

BRENDAN   I've as good a right to ordain priests as the Cardinal. It's only the difference of the Cardinal getting paid for it.

RIVERS   Marlowe said he had as good a right to mint money as the Queen of England. Did you know that?

BRENDAN   I did. And I'm glad someone else knows it, too.

WELSH WARDER   (Enters; blows his whistle) Garden Party! Turn to! On the double! One, two!
      (The boys form up and march around. As they do, they collect hoes from the warder and sing "The Borstal Song")

BORSTAL BOYS
      Oh, they say I ain't no good 'cause I'm a Borstal Boy,
      But a Borstal Boy is what I'll always be.
      I know it is a title, a title I bear with pride,
      To Borstal, to Borstal, and the beautiful country-
            side!
      I turned my back upon the 'ole society
      And spent me life a-thievin' 'igh and low,
      I've got the funniest feelin' for 'alf-inchin' and for
            stealin'

I should 'ave been in Borstal years ago, cor blimey!
I should 'ave been in Borstal years ago!
> *(The lighting goes up. The boys are now in open fields, bright sunlight. The warder blows his whistle. They start to dig)*

BEHAN My old man told me about the land and how our ancestors came from it and how healthy it was. So I asked my grandmother, and she said she was my ancestor and that all our family's land was in window boxes.

BRENDAN Charlie, I can smell the sea!
> *(He sings)*

The sea, oh, the sea, *a ghradh gheal mo chroidhe*,
Oh, long may you roll between England and me,
God help the poor Scotchmen, they'll never be free,
But we're entirely surrounded be water.

BORSTAL BOYS Good old Paddy!

CHEWLIPS *(Proudly)* 'E's a comical bastard, 'n't 'e?
> *(The warder blows his whistle. The boys look at him, puzzled)*

WELSH WARDER Well, fall out!
> *(The boys break off work and sit around. They begin to roll cigarettes and light up. BRENDAN finds himself beside KEN JONES)*

BRENDAN *(To KEN)* Have you no snout?

KEN No, Paddy. Smoked mine all up.

BRENDAN   Have some of mine.
   (*He gives* KEN *a cigarette paper and tobacco*)

CHARLIE   Didn't you get no snout, then?

KEN   I bought ten Woodbines. I don't like them much, but at least they're tailor-made. I don't fancy these things. I'm not a cowboy.

CHARLIE   None of us aren't cowboys. But if we're only getting fivepence or sixpence a week, this 'alf ounce snout lasts longer.
   (*He gets up and leaves them for another group*)

JOE   (*Calling after* CHARLIE *in a public-school voice*)   I 'eard my old man say the Woodbine is the dearest smoke there is—and the most expensive tobacco.

KEN   (*Ignoring* JOE)   Thanks for the smoke, Paddy.

BRENDAN   You're welcome.
   (JOE *moves off in mock disgust*)

KEN   I'll send you in some from the outside, Paddy, when I get out.

BRENDAN   Sure, kid.

KEN   You think I'm geeing you, Paddy, and that it'll be a long time before I'm on discharge. (*He drops his voice*) But I'm not going to wait for that.

BRENDAN   No?

KEN. No. I got it all worked out on a map I got in the

library. My brother will come up here and pick me
up in his Jaguar. He's a smashing driver, Paddy, and
an officer in the Marines.

BRENDAN Well, of course, if you could do it, if you
could get away with it.

KEN We'll be fifty miles away in the Jag before they
even start looking for me. You don't think I'm
kidding, do you?

BRENDAN No, Ken, I don't, of course I don't.

KEN I've got a pair of overalls planted and I'm going
to fall out during this break.

BRENDAN Maybe, kid, it would be better if you waited
till later. You'd have the whole night before you
then.

KEN No, I wouldn't. There's a watchman goes 'round
winding a clock every hour. They'll expect me to
make for the main road, but I'm way ahead of them
there, Paddy, you'll see.

BRENDAN Here, you'll need some snout. (*He passes* KEN
more tobacco) And here's some matches.

KEN Thanks, Paddy. You're a decent fellow. More than
I can say for these others. Some people don't like the
Irish—I do.

BRENDAN We're very popular among ourselves.

KEN You're a funny bloke, Paddy. Well, goodbye.

BRENDAN   Good luck, Ken, and God go with you.

BEHAN   It was sad—like seeing someone off to America.
(KEN *approaches the* WELSH WARDER)

KEN   Fall out, sir?

WELSH WARDER (*To* KEN)   Why don't you blokes put a
washer on it? Go on, then. (KEN *exits. The warder
blows his whistle*) Break up—back to work, come on,
yew shower, bend those backs like a leetle jackknife.

BEHAN   Ken was dead lonely. More lonely than I, and
with good reason. The other lads might give me the
rub about Ireland or about the bombing campaign,
and that was seldom enough, and I was never short
of an answer—historically informed and obscene. But
I was nearer to them than they would ever let Ken be.

CHARLIE   What did you give that Kensington puff a bit
of snout for?

BRENDAN   Because he hasn't anything to smoke and I
was reared that way be me mother, who would never
see anyone go without a smoke.

CHARLIE   Bloody college boy.

BRENDAN   Well, sure he has to do his time like anyone
else, no matter what he is.
(*They go on working*)

BEHAN   I had the same rearing as most of them—Dublin,
Liverpool, Manchester, Glasgow, London. All our
mothers had done the pawn—pledging on Monday,

releasing on Saturday. But Ken they never would accept. In a way, as the middle class and the upper class in England spend so much money and energy in maintaining the difference between themselves and the working class, Ken was only getting what his people paid for.

(He goes out)

CHARLIE   What's happened to your china with the old school tie?

BRENDAN   What about him?

CHARLIE   He hasn't come back from the loo yet. Where's 'e gone?

BRENDAN   I haven't got him in my fecking pocket.

CHARLIE   No need to take the needle for nothing.

BRENDAN   I'm not taking the needle, but you keep on about this bloke.

CHARLIE *(Shaking his head in temper)*   Oh, hump off, you, you just about got me brassed off. A bloke can't ask you a simple question. Sod off with your sodding college-boy china, then, and 'ave 'im for a china, and sod you.

BRENDAN   And sod you, too. And your friends in America and double-sod you.
    (The warder comes down, checking the prisoners and frowning)

WELSH WARDER   Where's your mate, Behaun?

BRENDAN You mean that lad that was working beside me, sir? In the next row, there?

WELSH WARDER Yes, and don't you come the old soldier, Behaun. You know bloody well who I mean.

BRENDAN He fell out at break, sir.

WELSH WARDER "He fell out at break, sir." I know bloody well he fell out at break, but where the hell is he now? *(Shouts)* Jones! Jones! *(Louder still)* Jo-o-ones.
   (He hurries off, blowing his whistle)

CHEWLIPS *(Excited)* Scarper, did 'e?

WELSH WARDER *(Offstage)* Jones! Jo-o-nes! Hey, Jones!

BORSTAL BOYS Hear that? Jones! Ken Jones! Scarpered! Taken a powder! Blimey! Humped off! Blown!
   (The boys gather around in great excitement)

CHARLIE I'm sorry I was so leery with you, Paddy. You knew he was scarpering, didn't you?

BRENDAN Of course I knew. But I couldn't tell you that, and the screw only a few yards from us.

CHARLIE You were dead right. I wouldn't like to grass on a bloke, neither. I suppose he goes to that bleedin' Sherwood Forest if they get him.

CHEWLIPS With Robin 'Ood and 'is merry men.

JOE No, not Jones. *(Slowly)* 'E's doing His Majesty's Pleasure.

CHARLIE   That's murder, isn't it?

HARTY   Yeh! *(Nodding)* One of the lucky ones. The judge said 'e'd 'ave 'ad 'im 'anged, but for 'is age.

CHARLIE   Cor!

HARTY   Most brutal murder and all that lot. 'E pushed 'is crippled brother's bath chair over a cliff.

BRENDAN   His brother's bath chair?

HARTY   With the brother in it.

BRENDAN   Jaysus.

JOE   Paralyzed or somethin', 'e was, from birth.

BRENDAN   How many brothers had he?

JOE   Only the one if y'ask me—I didn't know the family. Shouldn't bloody want to, neither.

WELSH WARDER *(Enters and blows his whistle)*   Come on, line up, look sharp. Now, get a move on. Don't be all day about it! Move!

CHEWLIPS *(Mischievously, to the warder)*   Fall out, sir? *(The warder chases him off)*

BORSTAL BOYS *(Singing as they march around and exit)*
    We're 'ere in Hollesley prison, fine Borstal Boys are we,
    We're not down yet for discharge, but we're waiting patiently.

79

And when it comes upon us, as it comes upon us all,
This chorus we will sing for you in South 'Ouse
    dining hall.
"Goodbye to dear old Borstal, goodbye to this old
    shack!
No more we'll see ya, Hollesley, for we're never
    coming back!"

JOCK *(Singing, very sad)*
    Ken Jones is never coming back!
    (The lights dim. It is now night. KEN JONES *is
    brought in by another warder and a man with a
    shotgun)*

WELSH WARDER Doesn't seem such a good idea now,
eh? Scarperin', I mean.

OTHER WARDER It's the Governor and chokey for you,
lad.
    *(The boys congregate at the back of the stage,
    whispering)*

CHEWLIPS Old Jonesy didn't make out, eh Pad?

BRENDAN I'd sooner it was him than me, kid.

CHARLIE Doesn't look so bleedin' 'ot, does he?

BRENDAN Give us a bit o' snout for him.

CHARLIE For 'im? For that college puff?

BRENDAN Come on. He's been out in that rain all night.

HARTY And 'e'll get chokey till 'is 'air falls out!
    (CHARLIE reluctantly parts with a butt)

CHARLIE   I'm not in the bloody Salvation Army.

JOE   He's no china of ours.

BRENDAN   We're all chinas when we're in trouble. Come on. (BRENDAN *approaches* KEN. *The warders pretend not to notice*) Well, Lamb of God, if it's not yourself.

KEN *(Almost in tears)*   Hello, Paddy.

BRENDAN   The dead arose and appeared to many. Where did you drop out of at all, at all.

KEN   I almost made it, Pad! Just bad luck.

BRENDAN   Sure, kid. Could happen to a bishop!

KEN   Wish to God I'd been caught sooner. *(Sobs)* I thought that with the overalls on me and the big boots the bus conductor would take me for a farm laborer.

BRENDAN   Ah, sure, God give you sense.

JOE   As much chance of 'em takin' me for Anthony Eden.

KEN   Instead, the bastard brought me to the cop shop.

JOE   He had you tumbled all the time. It was on the nine o'clock news.

A WARDER *(Blows his whistle, enters and calls)*   The Governor!
      (The boys start to run off)

GOVERNOR (*Enters*) Boys! Boys! There you are! What did I tell you? Nobody ever succeeds in scarpering. Walk out any time day or night. Who's to stop you? But you saw what happened to Jones. Thank God he didn't steal anything, anyway—or I'd be told off by the people living around the place. You'd almost think I'd done the stealing. So now, look, boys, don't sneak off without telling me.

(*They all go out. The lights dim to almost total darkness. There is a bugle call*)

VOICE ON P.A. SYSTEM (*Offstage*) Five-three-nine, Behan ... Five-three-three, Smith ... Five-three-nine, Behan ... Five-three-three, Smith. Report to engineers' yard at once ... Report to engineers' yard at once.

(WARDER O'SHEA *has entered in the dark; the lights come up on him.* BRENDAN *and* JOCK *appear and then run off as he sees them*)

O'SHEA Behan. I want you. You too, Smith! On the double! (BRENDAN *and* JOCK *come in*) I see you two fellows want to leave the Garden Party.

BRENDAN and JOCK (*Together*) That's right, sir.

O'SHEA You don't like it?

JOCK It's not that, sir. We're more used to building work, sir.

BRENDAN I was a painter in Dublin. It's not that we don't like working, but—

O'SHEA The old blarney. Well, fair exchange is no robbery. We're getting two lads that want to be transferred to the gardens. So they'll be coming down to us and you'll be reporting to the engineers' yard.

BRENDAN   Thank you, sir.

O'SHEA   Don't thank me, thank the Lord.
   (He goes)

BRENDAN   Imagine getting into overalls again.

JOCK   A real building job.

BRENDAN   Just like outside.

JOCK   Well, it's nearly the same as being outside. Old dolls up in the quarters, screws' wives making cups of tea for you, and all that. And there's two young maids in one big house we're going to. *(Digs* BRENDAN *in the ribs)* They'd eat it.

BRENDAN   Would they?

JOCK   Yes, a bloke called Yorky Turner got done over one of them. Six months they gave him.

BRENDAN   They might as well have left him alone. Nature breaks out in the eyes of a cat.

JOCK   It broke out in him, anyway. They let no one near the big house now. Only the plumber or the painter.

BRENDAN   Good openings for willing lads.
   (He sings)
   . . . Oh, there was the plumber in the servants' hall,

D'you think, oh me dear, he's going to solder us
all?
(JOE, RIVERS *and* HARTY *come in*)

JOE   What about us, then? Why ain't we given a chance
to follow our trade in 'ere, eh?
(BRENDAN *and* JOCK *burst out laughing*)

JOCK   Go away, you registered pimp.

JOE *(Feigning rage)*   And a better bloody trade than
yours or Paddy's. It's a diabolical liberty. Geezers get
no chance to follow their trade. 'Ere's me, I get no
chance whatso-bleedin'-ever to keep my 'and in.

BRENDAN   Your hand in what, Joe? *(Charlie comes in,
carrying his bedding)* Where are you going with that,
china?

CHARLIE *(Indignantly)*   You and me ain't chinas. You
go and work with Jock, and get Jock to put 'is bleedin'
kip next to yours, and all. You go anywhere you
bloody like, you and that bleedin' Jock.
(He totters off)

BRENDAN *(Looking after him)*   What can't be cured
must be endured.
*(The navvy gang, with wheelbarrow and picks
and shovels, come on.* CHEWLIPS, TOM, CRAGG *and*
SHAGGY *are among them)*

CHEWLIPS *and* TOM *(Singing)*
One, two, three, four,
Hitler has only got one ball,
Goering has two, but very small.

Himmler has something similar
And poor old Goebbels has no balls at all.

JOCK *(To* BRENDAN*)*   We don't go with them. We report
to the painter-in-charge and the plumber-in-charge.

BRENDAN *(Crossing himself)*   Thanks be to God we're
not going with that bunch.

JOCK   Say, blokes, do you know where we might find
the painter-in-charge and the plumber-in-charge?
(The navvies eye him in silence for a moment)

CRAGG   What do you want them for?

JOCK   Well, me and Paddy are working with them and
we want to get our tools and brushes.
*(A roar of laughter from the navvies. They shriek
and splutter, clapping each other on the back.
WARDER O'SHEA rushes back in)*

O'SHEA *(Roaring)*   Kip in, you shower. *(They fall in-
stantly silent. He rounds on* JOCK *and* BRENDAN*)* Where
the bloody 'ell do you pair think you're wandering
to?

BRENDAN   We're—looking for the painter and plumber.

CRAGG *(Shouting)*   Please, sir, the Jock says they're looking for their tools and brushes.
*(The navvies fall into an even louder explosion
of laughter than the first)*

O'SHEA *(Waving his arms)* Sharrap! Sharrap, I'm telling you.
>
> *(They do, for a second)*

SHAGGY Tell them they can have a loan of mine!
> *(They all burst out laughing again. The warder shouts; he goes unheeded. Now he lunges at them in a real temper)*

O'SHEA *(Roaring)* For the last time, keep shut, you shower! *(He turns back to* JOCK *and* BRENDAN*)* You'll get your tools and brushes. You'll get your tools out of the box like anyone else—a pick and shovel and—

SHAGGY *(Wheeling in a barrow)* A bloody big barrer!
> *(They burst into laughter again)*

O'SHEA I've warned you shower for the last time. You two get in line there, and I'll fix you up with brushes and tools. A wet day in the place and you think you're going to walk into a detached job. Wonder you don't get after the bloody padre's job. You shift enough shite out of that bloody big 'ole we got up 'ere, and throw down enough concrete, and barrow enough earth, and 'ave a bit more manners than this bloody shower—and then we'll see about brushes and tools. In six months time maybe. *(He roars)* Garden Party! *(Gestures to them to go)* And you there, put out that snout. Put it out or I'll put your bloody lights out! Quick march!
> *(O'SHEA goes out)*

BORSTAL BOYS *(March off, singing)*
> We are the nite shite shifters, we shift shite by night.

86

We shift muck, we shift dirt, and sometimes we shift—sweet violets . . .
(An Italian PRIEST *has entered, carrying a missal)*

PRIEST   You're the new Irish boy.

BRENDAN   Well, I'm not all that new, Father, but I'll do.

PRIEST   You're a Catholic, then?

RRENDAN   Am I?

PRIEST *(Surprised)*   Aren't you?

BRENDAN   Yes, Father.

PRIEST   Good. And I see you're a singer.

BRENDAN   The divil a one better.

PRIEST   I need a server.

BRENDAN   You mean a Mass server, Father?

PRIEST   Yes. You can serve Mass, can't you?

BRENDAN   Of course I can. But—I'm excommunicated.

PRIEST   Excommunicated? I don't understand. By whom? When?

BRENDAN   The bishops . . . both the Irish and the English sort. I'm in the I.R.A. and the bishop of this diocese won't let me have the sacraments because I question the right of his country to rule mine.

87

PRIEST   Remember, when you serve Mass, you do not serve me or the bishop. You serve God. Take the missal. You must try not to be bitter.
(*He goes out*)

BEHAN (*Has entered*)   Bitter? (*He shrugs*) Walton Jail scalded my heart with regard to my religion, but it also lightened it. My sins had fallen from me because I had almost forgotten there were such things. And when I got over it—my expulsion from religion—it was like being pushed outside a prison and told not to come back.

BRENDAN   Look at me now. Serving Mass.

BEHAN   If you're willing to serve Mass, it is in memory of our ancestors standing around a rock, in a lonely glen, for fear of the English landlords and their yeomen.
(BRENDAN *stands a moment in reflection; then* JOE, JOCK, HARTY *and* SHAGGY *come on*)

JOE   You're going to serve Mass, Pad?

BRENDAN   That's what the man said.

JOE   You got to go out a bit tasty like.
(*The boys prepare* BRENDAN *for serving Mass.* CRAGG *enters*)

JOE   You should have shaved again like I told you, Pad. (*He inspects* BRENDAN'*s chin*) This is one Mass I'm not going to miss.

HARTY   If we missed Mass on Sundays, my dad would

beat our mum. She told us Catholics worshiped the devil, but she got on 'er knees to us to go because 'e'd give 'er a kicking if she didn't, so we went because 'e'd kick 'ell out of us too.
    (There is a moment of sympathetic silence)

JOCK   Tell you what, Harty, can you run 'im through the Latin?

HARTY   Me? Not bloody likely. I can 'ardly read English.

JOCK   What about you, Cragg?

JOE   'E shouldn't be 'ere at all. 'E's an atheist, 'e is.

CRAGG   That's years ago, you silly-born bastard, when I was in Durham Prison. The padre wore robes at service, and 'e came into the condemned cell—

HARTY *(in a whisper)* 'E was in the condemned cell in Durham.

CRAGG   —and 'e asked me if I knew the significance of the different colors. I said I didn't but 'e should keep with the violet ones—they suited 'im. 'E did look well in them, though, that's truth . . . My wife came on a visit once!

JOE   Don't know what she ever saw in that dossy puff. Two nice kids, too. She comes two 'undred miles 'ere every month to see 'im.

CRAGG   Even though I croaked 'er old man.
    (There is silence. BRENDAN *looks at* CRAGG *in astonishment)*

89

HARTY   Go on with what you were tellin' Paddy about the padre.

CRAGG   Ah, 'e asks me 'ow I was getting on with my wife, so I said we were getting along champion, and I asks 'im 'ow 'e was getting on with 'is and was 'e keeping 'er off the old rum bottle, and 'e looks at me like I should 'ave been 'ung, too, and maybe I should, and I wouldn't 'ave minded neither, only it's so bloody painful. They used to 'ave religious texts on the wall of the condemned cell in Durham that Chaplain 'ad put there. One of them said, "Today is the morrow you worried about yesterday and nothing's 'appened." It was the last thing a bloke saw as 'e went out to be hanged.
    (He leaves. They are all silent)

JOCK   Come on and we'll run Paddy through 'is Latin. I'll do it. *In . . . tro . . . ibo . . . ad . . .*
    (CHARLIE *enters*)

JOE   Call that Latin? 'Ere, give me that. Come on, Pad. *Introibo ad altare Dei.*

BRENDAN   *Ad Deum qui laetificat juventutem meam.*

CHARLIE *(Sulking over a cigarette, at being left out)*
    Muttering there, like a set of bleeding witch doctors.

JOCK   Well, it's one thing in our Church: no matter where you go, the service is the same.

JOE   That's right, you go in a Catholic Church anywhere in the world and it's the same language.

CHARLIE   Well, they're all bleeding foreigners.

JOCK   And at every minute of the day, somewhere in the world a Mass is being said.

CHARLIE   'Ow about the North Pole? I reckon in the C. of E. at least you know what the bloke is saying.

JOE   Well, seein' as 'e's usually saying feck all, that shouldn't be hard. The C. of E. ain't a religion at all. They allow divorce and every fecking thing. They only got started because they allowed the King to 'ave a divorce when the Pope wouldn't 'ear of it.

BRENDAN
       "Don't speak of the alien minister
       Nor of his Church without meaning nor faith,
       For the foundation stone of his temple
       Is the balls of Henry the Eighth!"
That's what a preacher said in Ireland four hundred years ago.

CHARLIE   'E must 'ave been a lovely preacher to come out with language like that in church.
       (*The Mass bell sounds*)

BRENDAN   There's the bell. See you after Mass, Charlie.

CHARLIE   Maybe.
       (*He goes; then* SHAGGY)

BORSTAL BOYS   Good luck, Pad! Don't let us down! Up the High Hor Ay!
       (*The lights grow dim.* BRENDAN *advances alone, as if to the altar. We hear the voice of the* PRIEST)

91

PRIEST *(Offstage)* *Introibo ad altare Dei.*

BRENDAN *Ad Deum qui laetificat juventutem meam.*

BEHAN To God, Who giveth joy to my youth.

PRIEST *(Offstage)* To thee, O God, my God, I will give praise upon the harp.

BEHAN Why art thou sad, O my soul, and why dost thou disquiet me? I know what you're thinking, kneeling there murmuring the responses . . . You're thinking of the mother singing, "In that dread hour when in my bed I'm lying," while she scrubbed hell out of the washboard, and of Grandmother, shaking a pinch of snuff to her nostril during the sermon, and of old Sister Monica, telling us to go asleep with our arms folded so that if we died in the night, we'd have the sign of the cross on us.

> (BRENDAN *genuflects and crosses himself. The lights change. There is a sudden commotion and* BRENDAN *is in the middle of the boys.* CHARLIE *and* SHAGGY *enter)*

JOE Pad was smashing. Nearly better than the priest! There was that young puff of a college boy, and Paddy 'ad 'im down every time. Paddy worked the priest the wine and all—left this college boy with the water.

CHARLIE You could show a lot of these bastards up— these bleedin' college boys we get 'ere.

HARTY Will there be another Mass tomorrow?

JOCK Every morning. And Stations of the Cross on Friday.

JOE (*Exultantly*) All this arsin' 'round the chapel will be as good as a trip to Switzerland or a cruise in the Mediterranean.

CHARLIE (*Resentfully*) You lucky bastards. You'll be going down every afternoon from the mailbag room. You and Joe and Jock and Harty.

JOE That's right. You blokes can stop in the mailbag room and carry on with the seaming and bottoming and siding and roping while we'll be going down to the R.C. chapel and back. It's your own fault you're not coming. It's because you're a bloody 'eathen.

CHARLIE (*Indignantly*) I'm not a bloody 'eathen. I'm Church of England.

BRENDAN Don't mind Joe, he's only taking the piss.

CHARLIE 'E's got no call to go calling me a bloody 'eathen, even if he is only taking the piss.

SHAGGY (*Generously*) I don't see why he can't come.

HARTY No, I don't see why he can't come.

CHARLIE It's because I'm not a Roman Catholic. The screw will fall in only the R.C.'s.

JOE The screw won't know what number 'e's to get the first day, and after that, once 'e gets the same number, 'e won't care.

CHEWLIPS (*Enters. Shyly*) Can I—can I come, too, Paddy?

(They all turn to CHEWLIPS *with surprise, and study him)*

BRENDAN   You want to come to the R.C. services every day?

CHEWLIPS *(Anxiously)*   It'd be smashin', Paddy.

JOE *(To* CHEWLIPS)   You don't want to ask 'im. What do you think 'e is, the bleedin' Pope?

CHEWLIPS   Well, I'd just like to . . . matter of fact, I think I was inside a church only once. It's very interesting.

JOE *(Proudly)*   And this is different to the one you go to on Sunday. It's got candles, and . . . and incense, and . . . the lot.

CHEWLIPS   What's incense?

BRENDAN   It's a kind of smoke with perfume in it.

CHEWLIPS   Cor, smashing. Like the Jews.

CHARLIE   What's on this evening?

JOCK   Stations of the Cross.
(The chapel bell rings. The lights grow dim, and the boys arrange themselves uncertainly, genuflect awkwardly, and grow confused when making the sign of the cross. CHEWLIPS *kneels, facing the wrong way.* BRENDAN *sets him right.* CHEWLIPS *faces the altar. He reaches out for it*

*and gasps, "Cor, Chewlips!" BRENDAN pulls him
back. The organ begins to play "Stabat Mater."
The WELSH WARDER is looking on)*

BEHAN 'Round the Stations we went, and the little
Italian priest gave us a long and sorrowful account of
the agony in the garden and of Our Lord's betrayal
by Judas. Chewlips followed this with breathless
attention and muttered some comments about
Judas.

CHEWLIPS Bleedin' grass'opper!

PRIEST *(Offstage)* And Jesus said to him, "Judas, dost
thou betray the Son of Man with a kiss?"

CHEWLIPS *(Greatly agitated, to BRENDAN)* Just like
me, bleedin' bastard. We're going 'round into Rus-
sell Street and—

CHARLIE *(In a fierce whisper)* Kip in, you'll get us
done.
    (The warder is giving them very hard looks)

PRIEST *(Offstage)* And they that were about Him, seeing what would follow, said to Him, "Lord, shall we
strike with the sword?"

CHEWLIPS *(Jumping up)* That's it—carve the bastard
up!
    (The others pull him back)

CHARLIE Shahrrrapp! That screw has you copped.
    (The others now mime what BEHAN is describing)

BEHAN The padre was most upset about Our Lord's Holy Passion and how he was taken in the Garden of Olives by the other crowd on information received, having been shopped by Judas and then taken off and most cruelly flogged. Joe was there in the middle, shouting the "Stabat Mater" and "Whose sorrow is like unto mine?"—and his hands deep in Shaggy's pocket and he comes up with a whole cigarette and big dogend. And there is old Cragg, exploring a bag he's just taken out of someone's pocket, and he hands me a piece of jelly from it, which I stick into my mouth and swallow in one delicious gulp. Joe gets a light for his butt off Jock, and there are plenty of lads in the middle of the congregation smoking, but the screws can't tell cigarette smoke from incense. There is Harty leaning against a statue of St. Jude, the Patron of Hopeless Cases, reading a *News of the World,* and two of the chokey blokes savaging sandwiches, and Shaggy for dessert eating a Mars bar and looking over at the priest and the crowd 'round the picture as if he thought very well of them.

JOE *(To* CHARLIE) What do you think of it, Tosh?

CHARLIE *(Chewing)* Smashing, ain't it?

CHEWLIPS I reckon 'e's finishing up now.

BRENDAN So he is.

JOCK We better scarper back. Ta for now.

JOE Ta.

CHARLIE Ta.

BRENDAN We'll see you tomorrow—with the help of God. Come on, Chewlips.

> *(They all go out, except* CHEWLIPS, BRENDAN *and the warder)*

WELSH WARDER *(Pounces on* CHEWLIPS*)* Now, when were you converted?

CHEWLIPS Eh—wot—sir?

WELSH WARDER You're not a Roman Catholic.

CHEWLIPS *(Gulping)* No, sir. But my gran was an R.C. and always eat fish on Friday.

WELSH WARDER *(Menacingly)* You and your gran, eh?

CHEWLIPS And taters. *(Trailing off)* She'd eat buckets of fish and taters . . .

WELSH WARDER *(To* BRENDAN*)* And you knew he wasn't a Catholic, Behaun.

BRENDAN It's all equal to me what he is. I don't own the Church.

WELSH WARDER I don't want any of your old buck, Behaun. You'll behave yourself in church and not be talking and whispering and laughing. Now, off with you. *(He turns back to* CHEWLIPS. BRENDAN *leaves)* You don't come again, understand? Now come and explain yourself to the officer of the mailbag class.

> *(*CHEWLIPS *genuflects primly once more. The warder hustles him off.* BEHAN *enters and sings as the boys bring on and set the beds for the dormitory)*

97

BEHAN *(Sings)*
Now, Borstal is a lovely place,
At nighttime there they wash your face.
"Good night, my son," the screw will say,
"There ends another happy day!"
There's a screw to tuck you into bed,
And lay a pillow 'neath your head.
And as you lie there fast asleep,
'E'll plant a kiss right on your cheek!
(BEHAN exits)

BORSTAL BOYS *(Sing)*
Right on your cheek.
(BRENDAN runs in)

CHARLIE   Hi—there 'e is now. Where've you been, Pad?

BRENDAN   Talking to the other altar boy. He's an Irishman—I.R.A. He worked me some snout.
(They all gather around BRENDAN)

CHEWLIPS   Cor! The I.R.A. worked the snout and chocolates in for you.

SHAGGY   Old Paddy's got snout.

HARTY   Another R.I.A. man worked it to 'im.

JOE   Tain't R.I.A. It's I.R.A., ain't it, Paddy?

CHARLIE   Wohzamarafawghwohihis, if it's I.R.A. or R.A.F., so long as 'e's got the snout.

HARTY   Dog-ends on you, Paddy.

SHAGGY Hey, bugger off. I was dog-ends on 'im first.

CHARLIE *(Indignantly)* Hump off, you puffs, 'is chinas come first.

SHAGGY Don't tell me to 'ump off, you silly-born bastard, or I shall go over there and bloody pop you one.

CHARLIE You bloody well won't, you know.

BRENDAN For the love of Jaysus, keep easy, or none of us will get a bash. The screw will be 'round. There's enough for everybody. Here, Charlie. Here, Shaggy.
(He distributes cigarettes and candy)

SHAGGY *(Offering CRAGG some)* Here, Cragg.

CRAGG Hump off, you lot. I'm improving me mind.

JOCK Say, Cragg, what are you reading?

CRAGG *The Decline and Fall of the Roman Empire.* Not for you blokes.

JOCK Read us a wee bit. *(The others protest)* Go on.

CRAGG "Such was the depravity of the times that she preferred the timorous touchings of the eunuch to the ponderous ballocks of the Roman Emperor."
(Several boys exclaim and run to look at the book)

BRENDAN I never knew *The Decline and Fall of the Roman Empire* had such interesting things in it.

RIVERS Ever read this, Paddy?

BRENDAN *(Reads the title)* *The Life of Oscar Wilde* by Frank Harris. *(Eagerly)* I was born only a few hundred yards from where Wilde was born.

RIVERS Oh?

BRENDAN I used to think Wilde was sent to the nick for being an Irish patriot. But I believe now it was over sex.

RIVERS And you don't know what he was really in for?

BRENDAN Well, not exactly.

RIVERS I'll show you exactly, *(Shows him a page.* CHEW-LIPS *looks, too; says, "Cor")* Well, what do you think of your *wild* Irishman, now?

BRENDAN I think that every cripple has his own way of dancing, and I think that if that shocks you, it's just as well ordinary people didn't hear about it. Because, bejaysus, if it shocked you, it'd turn thousands gray.

JOE The best book I ever saw in the nick was the Bible.

CHARLIE 'Ark at 'im. The Bible!

JOE Smashing thin paper for rolling fags in. I must 'ave smoked my way through the Book of Genesis before I went to court.

JOCK Ssh! Here comes the screw!
(All dive into bed. WARDER O'SHEA *enters with a flashlight. He shines the light on each bed in turn)*

O'SHEA   Hey you! Hey you! *(Shouts)* Hey you! *(CHEW-LIPS struggles awake)* Dormitory captain! *(RIVERS gets up and comes to O'SHEA and stands with the warder at the foot of CHEWLIPS' bed)* Who is this fellow? Get 'im out of it. *(RIVERS shakes CHEWLIPS)* Come on, out of it! Throw him out of it! *(CHEWLIPS slowly and fearfully gets up and stands next to the bed)* Come on, get them off. *(CHEWLIPS starts to take off his shirt)* Your bloody socks! *(He points to CHEWLIPS' feet, which are still in stockings pulled up over his pajamas in the manner of a cyclist)* Nice thing, and a bloody 'ouse captain in, and I 'ave to come in and find a fellow with 'is socks on in bed.

RIVERS   I'm sorry, sir.

O'SHEA   As long as I'm officer 'ere, I'll stand no man going to bed with 'is socks on, winter or summer. I don't care 'ow cold it is. It's not a 'ealthy 'abit and I'll get the man out of bed fifty times in the night if I suspect 'e's got anything on besides 'is pajamas. *(To CHEWLIPS)* Now, you remember that.
   (He leaves)

RIVERS   Bad show, Chewlips!

BORSTAL BOYS   Bloody bad show!
   (CHEWLIPS nods fearfully. RIVERS climbs back into bed. CHEWLIPS gets slowly back into bed and covers himself)

JOCK   Hey, Chewlips, that screw is dead nuts on anyone trying to sleep with 'is socks on.

CHEWLIPS *(Mournfully)* I wonder 'ow 'e knows I 'ad them on?

JOCK Why, you silly-born sod, when he didn't see them with your shoes under the bed he knew, didn't he?

CHEWLIPS I never thought of that. But if I did 'ave a pair under me bed, 'e wouldn't bother, would 'e?
   (CHEWLIPS *leaps from his bed, fetches some spare socks from under the pillow, puts them on, places the first pair in his shoes, hollers, "Foh- pance a pahnd—pehhs!" and leaps back into bed. The lights grow dim. In the darkness, voices call to* BRENDAN)

SHAGGY Thanks, Paddy, for the snout.

BRENDAN That's all right, kid, you're welcome.

BORSTAL BOYS *(Together)* Thanks, Paddy.

JOE Good night, Pad.

BRENDAN Good night, Joe. Good night, Charlie. Good night, Harty.

CHARLIE Good night, Joe. 'Night, Paddy.

CHEWLIPS Good night, Paddy—and Up the Hey R. Hey, or whatever you call it.
   (They all laugh in the dark)

BRENDAN Good night, Chewlips; good night, all.
   (They settle down for sleep. BEHAN *enters)*

BEHAN Reposed and innocent they look now, every mother's son of them, including myself. *(The lights change; a bugle blows—it is morning. The boys remove the beds—but* CHEWLIPS *is still sleeping in his bed. They call to him to wake up. Finally they all gather at his bed and shout together: "Rise and shine, the day is fine/ The sun will scorch your balls off!" They pick up his bed with him in it, and carry it off-stage as he sits up in bed and yells; "Foh-pance a pahnd—pehhs!"* TOM MEADOWS *enters during the following, carrying a ladder and paint pot and brush. He sets them down and commences to work)* Time passing is like a bank balance growing to a prisoner, and every day, week and month for pounds, shillings and pence. Though I was not thinking of discharge yet. It was a bit soon for that. But still, roll on. I got a detached job at last! No more of that goddamned navvy gang. Wondering every morning who you'll have to fight before the day is out!

(BRENDAN *enters)*

TOM Hello, Paddy.

BRENDAN *(Smiling)* Hello, Tom.

BEHAN Tom Meadows was the only other painter left on the skeleton staff while the rest were out fruit pickin'. Joe said he was the right one to leave on the skeleton staff 'cause he looked like a bleedin' skeleton.

TOM Do you know, Paddy, they're a bloody rum lot here, if you ask me, a bloody rum lot. I shan't be sorry when I get out again among decent, honest folk. *(He sighs)* Whenever that may be.

BRENDAN   Very soon, I hope, Tom, please God.

TOM   I don't 'old with the I.R.A., Paddy, but it's a disgrace to put you into Borstal among a lot of scum.

BRENDAN   Ah, sure, the blokes are only working-class kids like ourselves, Tom.

TOM *(Indignantly)*   They're not. They're not working-class blokes. They're reared up to thieving and stealing and living off prostitutes the same as the boss class. And they know it. If you ever hear them talking of any heroes outside the nick, it's about the way Anthony Eden dresses, or the way the Duke of Windsor ties a knot in 'is tie. 'Aven't you noticed nearly all thieves are Tories?

BRENDAN   Maybe it's because all Tories are thieves.

TOM   And you can't talk to these other daft bastards. They're too stupid, and when they 'ave owt to say, it's about filth and muck, when it's not shagging lies about all the millions of money they 'ave stacked away for when they get out. One fellow was 'ere, 'e 'ad me near driven barmy telling me about 'is spiv suits and about running about with 'oors in taxis.

BRENDAN *(Laughing as though he has to)*   By God, Tom, you never lost it. You don't care a damn what you say, but speak it right out of your mind. And do you know what I'm going to tell you? (BRENDAN *looks at him seriously*) You're bloody well right, too.

TOM *(Smiles deprecatingly)*   Well, Pad, we're blunt folk where I come from. (BRENDAN *starts the first line of*

a song. TOM *interrupts)* Know this one, Pad? *(He sings)*
   ... It looked around our infant might,
   When all beside looked dark as night,
   It witnessed many a deed and vow,
   We will not change its color now ...
     (BRENDAN *joins in)*

BRENDAN and TOM
   Then by this banner swear we all,
   To bear it onward till we fall,
   Come dungeons dark or gallows grim,
   This song will be our parting hymn—
   Then raise the scarlet standard high,
   Beneath its folds we'll live or die,
   Let cowards mock or traitors sneer,
   We'll keep the red flag flying here!
     (JOE, JOCK, CHARLIE *and* CHEWLIPS *limp on,*
     singing: "We are the nite shite shifters," holding
     their aching backs, and carrying forks. They
     collapse onto some benches. TOM *keeps well away*
     from them)

BEHAN   The four just men, home for their tea.

JOCK *(Looking at* TOM*)* Paddy and the head boy on
   the painters had a bleeding choir practice. Singing
   the whole evening, they were.

JOE *(So that* TOM *can't hear)* Hey, Paddy, come 'ere.
   Don't 'ave anything to do with that bloke. 'E's
   been in trouble with the police.

BRENDAN   In trouble with the police? Sure haven't we
   all been in trouble with the police?

JOE But 'e's the bleeding Lancashire strangler. Doing H.M.P. for croaking 'is judy—with 'er own stocking. She was going with some other bloke in 'er off-time.

CHEWLIPS Stuff me!

BRENDAN That accounts for his givin' out about you blokes!

JOCK And he wasn't married to her. It was bloody savage. She was only seventeen, and all.

BRENDAN It was a bit stern, all right.

JOCK Maybe she was knocked up. In Scotland, the old dolls in the place would never let you forget that.

BRENDAN And in Ireland, down the country anyway, if a girl got knocked up she might as well leave on the next boat or drown herself and have done with it. The people there are so Christian and easily shocked.

(The COOK *comes in, an old ex-army type, with a flagon of cider and some mugs)*

BEHAN The cook's name, by the way, in case I didn't mention it before, was Tucker. Humorously referred to as Tucker the—oh well, never mind.

(The COOK *gives out mugs of cider)*

BRENDAN Good old . . . Tucker!

COOK You're the Irish bloke, ain't you?

BRENDAN *(Nods)* That's right, and may the giving hand never falter. *(He sips)* It's like cider.

COOK   Like Guinness, ain't it? Ah, the old scrump. Know the way my old dad used to make it, Paddy?

BRENDAN   It's made from apples, ain't it?

COOK   'Course. All cider is made from apples. But not everyone can make it like everyone else, or as good.

BRENDAN   Stands to common sense, that does, like everything else.

COOK   Well, my old dad, when 'e 'ad the juice of the apples all pressed out and casked like, before 'e closed the cask 'e'd throw into the ten-gallon cask a quart of brandy, seven pounds of the best beef and a dead rat.
   (JOE, JOCK, CHARLIE *and* CHEWLIPS *spew out the cider and look at him in horror*)

BRENDAN (*Calmly*)   It must have been a recipe handed down.

COOK   That's what it was, Paddy, 'anded down. (*Pauses*) 'Course, rat, he was skinned.

JOCK (*Still spitting out cider*)   Jesus!
   (*He runs off, holding his mouth*)

COOK   Put them mugs up in the window sill when you've finished. I've got to get back to me soup.
   (*He goes into the kitchen*)

JOE   'Anded down. What was 'anded down, the bloody rat?

JOCK   He's a disgusting old bastard, and no mistake.

CHEWLIPS   I wonder how many he put in the soup. Four pence a pair—rats! *(The boys throw their cider in his face and go out)* What have I done now?
> *(He goes out too.* TOM MEADOWS, *who has been apart from all this, collects his paints, etc., and starts to leave)*

BEHAN *(Sings)*
> I had no mother to break her heart
> I had no father to take my part
> I had one friend and a girl was she . . .

And he croaked her with her own silk stocking . . . At Christmas, Matron put on a Nativity play. Harty and Joe were census takers. *(They enter)* Jock and Charlie were shepherds. *(They enter)* Chewlips was a wise man. *(He enters)* Ken Jones was St. Joseph. *(He enters and* BRENDAN *enters)* And believe it or not, Shaggy was a shagging angel. *(*SHAGGY *enters. They are all dressed in costumes for their various parts.* SHAGGY *crosses the stage, climbs a ladder and stands in an angelic attitude)* One of the screws' wives, a young girl, was to play the Virgin Mary.
> *(A stunning girl crosses the stage)*

WARDER'S WIFE   Cragg! Anyone seen Cragg?
> *(She exits)*

JOE *(Smitten)*   I want to be St. Joseph. I am Joseph anyway, always have been in real life.

BRENDAN   You'd be a bit too much like real life, Joe.

JOE   Well, then, I want to be the Holy Ghost.

JOCK   You silly-born twerp, there's no Holy Ghost in this play.

BRENDAN   Nick, nick, here she comes again.
   *(The "Virgin Mary" crosses back in, carrying a
   doll in a manger, smiles at all, and leaves)*

JOE *(Desperately)*   Well, then, I want to be the baby.
   (He runs after the girl. The boys trip him up)

SHAGGY   Rise up, Joseph.
   (They all rush off, chased by JOE)

BEHAN   That night we had a singsong, and they all
   shouted, "Paddy, give us a song!" So this is what I
   sang. *(Sings, with BRENDAN joining in betimes)*

   I took me girl up to the zoo
   To show her the lion and the kangaroo
   All she wanted to see was me oul' cockatoo
   Up in the zoological gardens.

   Thunder and lightning, it's no lark
   When Dublin City is in the dark
   If you have any money go up to the park
   And view the zoological gardens.

   Oh, says she, it's seven o'clock
   I have to go home for you've ruined me frock
   And I knew she was one of the rale oul' stock
   Up in the zoological gardens.

   Thunder and lightning, it's no lark
   When Dublin City is in the dark
   If you have any money go up to the park
   And view the zoological gardens.

   As we went up be the old park gate
   The policeman was upon his beat.
   He waves his baton at me darlin' Kate
   Outside the zoological gardens.

Thunder and lightning, it's no lark
When Dublin City is in the dark
If you have any money go up to the park
And view the zoological gardens.

We went up there on me honeymoon
Say she, me love, if you don't come soon
I'll have to get in with the hairy baboon
Up in the zoological gardens.

Thunder and lightning, it's no lark
When Dublin City is in the dark
If you have any money go up to the park
And view the zoological gardens.
(All the boys cheer offstage)

CHEWLIPS *(Shouting, offstage)*   You're a good kid, Paddy!

BEHAN   *A vico,** you're all good kids.

BRENDAN   We're all good kids. We're all the kids our
mothers warned us against.
(JOCK, HARTY, JOE, SHAGGY, *and* CHEWLIPS *enter
in civilian clothes, carrying luggage and singing)*

One more hour and we shall be,
Out of the dump of misery
Bye, bye, Borstal.

Out the door and we'll be free,
You'll see sweet feck-all of me,
Bye, bye, Borstal.

The Governor and the screws don't understand us,
All that Borstal bullshit they all hand us.

I've packed my bag and packed my grip,

* My son.

110

We're not coming back next trip,
Borstal—bye, bye!

(*As they go off*)
Goodbye, Pad! See you, Pad! Up the Hi! Har! Hey!

CHEWLIPS (*Sings*)
Foh-pance a pahnd—pehhs!
(CHARLIE *comes in slowly alone, in his sailor's uniform*)

BRENDAN   Begod, china, the Germans will be dead frit when they hear you're back in the crow's-nest.

CHARLIE   Oh, get stuffed, you bloody mad bomber. 'Eeere, what's that, something you nicked?

BRENDAN   If you weren't such a bloody heathen, Charlie, you'd know today's St. Patrick's Day, and this is shamrock. Here, I'll put it in your hat for luck.

CHARLIE (*Smiling*)   Pad, remember that song you used to sing in the summer, down by the beach?

BRENDAN (*Sings*)
The sea, oh, the sea, *a ghradh gheal mo chroidhe* . . .

CHARLIE   That's it! Well, listen, I've got a new way to sing it. (*Sings*)
The sea, oh the sea, *a ghradh gheal mo chroidhe*,
O long may you roll between *Borstal* and me!
(*They both laugh*)
They were smashin' days, down there last summer, Pad.

BRENDAN   They were and all, Charlie.

CHARLIE *(Extending his hand)* Goodbye, Pad.

BRENDAN Goodbye, Charlie.
  (Sings)
  Is go dtéighidh tú, a mhúirnín, slán.

CHARLIE Up the I.R.A.
  (He goes out slowly)

BEHAN *(After a pause)* Summer came again, and every day, there I was, going up the road to work, grown up now like Ossian after the Fianna. And then one October day—
  (WARDER O'SHEA comes in slowly)

O'SHEA Remember your china, Paddy?

BRENDAN Which of them? Is it Charlie Millwall?

O'SHEA *(Handing BRENDAN a cigarette and lighting it for him)* Yes. I just heard today in the mess. Millwall—

BRENDAN Charlie is dead.

O'SHEA You knew? You'd heard already?

BRENDAN Oh, I just fecking guessed. *(Pauses)* Where was it? At sea, I suppose.

O'SHEA Remember the convoy was attacked, and the *Southampton* was sunk a couple of weeks ago?

BRENDAN I suppose I do. I don't take that much interest in your bloody convoys, as a rule.

O'SHEA   Well, it was in the Straits of Gibraltar.

BRENDAN   I'd have guessed it—that he'd have been croaked before the end of the war.

O'SHEA   How's that?

BRENDAN *(He starts to answer, but changes his mind)* Thanks for telling us, Mr. O'Shea, and thanks for the bit of snout.

O'SHEA *(Pats* BRENDAN *on the shoulder)*   That's all right, Paddy boy.
    (He goes. BRENDAN *sits down, lost in thought)*

BRENDAN *(Sings softly)*
    Walk, walk, walk, my own,
    Not even God can make us one,
    Now you have left me here alone,
    Is go dtéighidh tú, a mhúirnín, slán.
        (He sits with his head bowed. The WELSH WARD-
        ER *enters and calls, "Behaun! Behaun!" He has a
        bucket and sandpaper. He is followed by* TOM,
        KEN, CRAGG, *and another boy. They all have
        buckets and sandpaper)*

WELSH WARDER   Now, Bee-haun, you'll clean this bucket till it's like silvair.

BRENDAN   I will in my ass.

WELSH WARDER   What is that you say, Bee-haun?

BRENDAN   I never saw a silver bucket in my whole bloody life.

WELSH WARDER   I'll show you. *(He takes a piece of sand-paper and begins polishing the bucket.* BRENDAN *looks at the bucket in mock idiocy. The* WARDER *throws it down in a temper)* All right, Bee-haun, I've just 'ed enuv off yew. You're for the Governor in the morning.

BRENDAN *(Mimicking)*   I'm not, yew know.

WELSH WARDER   Yew are for 'im in the morning.

BRENDAN   I'm not for him in the morning, or any other fecking time. And sod him, and sod you, too, you stringy-looking puff.
   (The warder is agape. He blasts furiously on his whistle. BRENDAN *grimaces behind his back. The boys are delighted, and laugh silently.* O'SHEA *comes on the run with another warder)*

O'SHEA   What's up, Mr. Hacknell?

WELSH WARDER   It's this Irish pig—

O'SHEA   Paddy? 'Ere, what's all this?

WELSH WARDER   He said sod me and sod the Governor and called me a stringy-looking puff!

O'SHEA *(Looking the warder up and down)*   Did you, Paddy?

BRENDAN   Yes, I did.

O'SHEA   It's chokey for him so! Come on, grab him—into the cell with him.

(The other two warders throw BRENDAN *into a cell. The lights dim, except for a light on* BRENDAN. *The* PRIEST *is in the shadows)*

BRENDAN To hell with you all! Leave me alone!

BEHAN Take it easy, son!

BRENDAN They're not going to pull that Walton stuff on me again!

BEHAN We won't forget Walton in a hurry, will we? Or the excommunication?
(The PRIEST *moves toward* BRENDAN)

BRENDAN Keep away from me, you fat bastard! You and your excommunication. I suppose you think excommunication is something new to the I.R.A. Wasn't my own father excommunicated? To hell with Rome! To hell with England! Up the Republic!
(The PRIEST *comes into the light)*

PRIEST Up the Republic every time, Brendan.

BRENDAN *(Dazedly)* There was a priest in Walton—

PRIEST Walton? You've come a long way from Walton, my son. And soon you'll be a long way from Hollesley Bay—back safe and sound in that Republic you love.

BRENDAN What?

PRIEST You're going out this morning, Brendan. We've known about it all week.
(The warders, the GOVERNOR *and the boys are*

*gathered around. The boys are cheering. The
lights come up)*

O'SHEA   That's right, Paddy. The Governor locked you
up to keep you out of trouble. The boys want to give
you a big cheer in the dining hall.
   (Cheers are heard offstage)

PRIEST *(Smiling)*   Well, my dear Brendan, what will I
do now for a Mass server?

BRENDAN   Get another I.R.A. man, I suppose.

PRIEST *(Earnestly)*   I wish I could hear your confession
before you go out—

BRENDAN *(Smiling)*   Only sinful people have to go to
confession.

BEHAN   It's only dirty people have to wash.

PRIEST   But His Lordship, the Bishop—

BRENDAN   That's all right, Father, I understand.

PRIEST   Well, my son, goodbye and good luck, and may
God bless you always.

BRENDAN *(Taking the* PRIEST's *proffered hand)*   And you
too, Father.

O'SHEA   Goodbye, Paddy.

GOVERNOR   Goodbye and good luck, Brendan.

116

BORSTAL BOYS Good old Paddy! Hooray for Pad! Up
the Hey! Ar! Hey! Good boy, Pad!
  (*All exit, except* BEHAN)

BEHAN (*Sings*)
  As I walk out of this lovely dump
  In my throat will come a great big lump,
  And I will gaze with eyes so full of tears
  At the place where I spent three 'appy years.

BORSTAL BOYS (*Offstage*) Some fecking 'opes!
  (BRENDAN *emerges, all dressed up in a new suit,
  shouting "Goodbye!" The boys offstage shout
  goodbyes*)

BEHAN . . . and I will make my journey, if life and
death but stand/Unto that pleasant country, that
fresh and fragrant strand/And leave your boasted
braveries, your wealth and high command/For the fair
hills of Holy Ireland . . . There they are, as if you'd
never left them, in their sweet and stately order 'round
the bay—the Dublin mountains and the spires and
the chimneys, all counted, present and correct, from
Bray head right 'round to Kilbarrack.

BRENDAN I can't really see Kilbarrack, but I know it's
there. So many belonging to us lie buried in Kilbarrack.

BEHAN The healthiest graveyard in Ireland because it's
so near the sea.
  (*There is the blast of a ship's whistle.* BRENDAN
  *searches in his pocket and brings out the expul-
  sion order. An* IMMIGRATION MAN *comes in. The*

117

crowds, with their luggage, move around, talking and laughing, covering BRENDAN *up for a moment)*

IMMIGRATION MAN   Passport, travel permit or identity document, please. *(*BRENDAN *hands him the document; he reads)* Behan, Brendan. *(Hands it back. He takes* BRENDAN's *hand) Cead mile failte abhaile romhat.* A hundred thousand welcomes home to you.

BRENDAN *(Smiling)   Go raibh maith agat.*

IMMIGRATION MAN *(Tenderly)   Caithfidh go bhfuil se go h-iontach bheith saor?*

BRENDAN   *Caithfidh go bhfuil.*

IMMIGRATION MAN   It must be wonderful to be free.

BRENDAN   It must.
    (He goes)

BEHAN   It must indeed ... *(Sings)*
    ... Is go dtéighidh tú, a mhúirnín slán ...

Curtain

About the Authors

BRENDAN BEHAN, one of the most colorful and controversial of recent Irish writers, was born in Dublin in 1923. At the age of fourteen he became a messenger for the Irish Republican Army. When he was sixteen, he was sent by the I.R.A. to blow up the shipyards at Liverpool. Arrested there, he was jailed and then sentenced to three years at a Borstal (reformatory for boys). It is these years that he vividly recorded in an autobiography of his late teens, *Borstal Boy* (1958), on which Frank McMahon's play is based. Brendan Behan's other books include a novel, *The Scarperers,* and a second autobiography, *Confessions of an Irish Rebel.* His two plays, *The Quare Fellow* (1956) and *The Hostage* (1958) enjoyed success in both London and New York. Brendan Behan died in Dublin in 1964 at the age of forty-one.

FRANK McMAHON is a native New Yorker who now makes his home in Ireland. After graduating from Fordham University, he served in the United States Navy in World War II. He has been an executive with NBC and MCA and most recently with Irish Television. At present, he runs his own publishing house in Dublin. *Borstal Boy,* his first play for the legitimate theater, has enjoyed the longest consecutive run in the seventy-year history of the Abbey Theatre, Dublin.

TOMÁS MACANNA, who originated the idea of dramatizing *Borstal Boy* and shaped Frank McMahon's adaptation into an award-winning play, is artistic director of the Abbey Theatre.